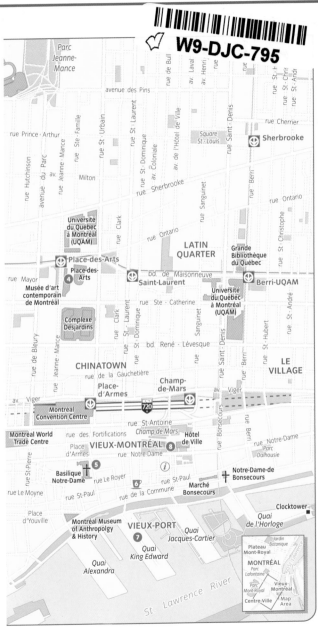

Tackling the major attractions of Montréal in one day may seem daunting, but follow the tour below and you'll be weaving your way through the bilingual boulevards of the city with surprising efficiency. Don't forget to slow down once in a while, or you'll miss the little street-side occurrences that make the city so enchanting—like the wafting aroma of freshly baked bagels from St-Viateur or the sounds of a saxophone busker on Rue Ste-Catherine. START: **Take the Métro to the Peel or Guy-Concordia station and walk along rue Sherbrooke ouest to the Musée des Beaux Arts.**

❶ ★★★ Musée des Beaux Arts.
Opened in 1912, the renowned Musée des Beaux Arts is home to more than 30,000 works ranging in style from French Impressionism to 20th-century modernism to contemporary Canadian. The newer Jean-Nöel Desmarais Pavilion, designed by noted Montréal architect Moshe Safdie, contains the bulk of the museum's collection of 12th- to 19th-century art—painted, sculpted, or sketched by such names as Brueghel, Renoir, Monet, Picasso, and Cezanne. Though the original building is home to incredible pieces, you're best off spending the majority of your visit in this modern addition. ⏱ *2 hr. Avoid coming here on the weekends. 1379–1380 rue Sherbrooke ouest.* ☎ *514/285-2000. www.mmfa.qc.ca. Free admission to permanent collection. Temporary exhibitions: C$15 adults, C$7.50 for seniors and students, C$30 for families (1 adult, 3 kids under 16; or 2 adults and 2 kids under 16), free for kids 12 and under. Tues 11am–5pm, Wed–Fri 11am–9pm, Sat–Sun 10am–5pm. Ticket counter closes 30 min. before museum closes. Métro: Peel or Guy-Concordia.*

The prices and ambience at the tiny, eclectic **❷ Architecture Café** reflect its status as one of the few student-run cafes at McGill University. Students bring their own mugs (there are paper cups for the unprepared) to this cozy little nook, where you can get a fresh cup of surprisingly tasty joe for C50¢ and other cafe fare (various pastries, scones) while kicking back on almost-antique furniture. *815 rue Sherbrooke ouest (in basement of McDonald-Harrington building). www.arch.mcgill.ca/asa/archcafe.html. $.*

Montréal's Musée des Beaux Arts is home to over 30,000 works.

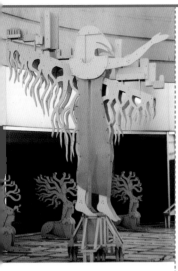

Sculpture at the Museum Contemporain.

3 McGill University/Redpath Museum. Prestigious McGill University, home to over 30,000 undergrads and graduate students, was born when, in 1813, Scottish merchant James McGill bequeathed the land it sits on for the creation of a "Royal Institution for the Advancement of Learning." Today the campus is a small green oasis among the austere office buildings and neon-lit malls that pervade downtown Montréal. Walk the campus's winding paths to admire its interesting collection of architectural styles—from the

Artifact from the Egyptian collection at the Redpath Museum.

modern Lorne Trottier building to the historic Arts Building. Also nestled inside the campus is the small, but noteworthy, Redpath Museum. Housed in a grand, 19th-century building, the museum is home to an intriguing Egyptian collection (second-largest in Canada) and a slew of fossils that draw lots of local elementary school kids on field trips. ⏱ *30 min. Rue Sherbrooke and Rue McGill College. www.mcgill.ca. Open daily. Free admission to museum. Museum open Mon–Fri 9am–5pm, Sun 1–5pm. Métro: McGill.*

4 ★★ Musée d'Art Contemporain de Montréal. The Canadian equivalent of New York's MoMa displays modern works of every conceivable style, from the 1940s to the present day. Though most of the permanent collection's works are the products of Québécois artists, there's also a fair amount of famous international names (such as Ansel Adams and Vik Muniz) to be found on the placards next to the paintings, sculptures, and photographs. Because new exhibitions arrive every few months, take advantage of the guided tours (Wed at 6:30pm and Sat–Sun at 1pm and 3pm) to get acquainted with the newest works. ⏱ *1½ hr. 185 rue Ste-Catherine ouest. ☎ 514/847-6226. www.macm.org. Admission (includes guided tour) C$8 adults, C$6 seniors, C$4 students, free for kids under 12, C$16 for families; free Wed 6–9pm. Open Tues–Sun 11am–6pm (until 9pm Wed); open Mon June 20–Sept 10. Métro: Place des Arts.*

5 ★★★ Basilique Notre Dame.

James O'Donnell, architect of this immense Catholic basilica (it can hold 4,000 worshippers), became its first parishioner though he was a Protestant when he began working on it. His creation (finished in 1824) was so breathtaking and moving that once it was completed, he quickly converted. While visitors may not be motivated to get baptized after their visit, they are usually taken aback by its sheer beauty. The ethereal lighting, gilded adornments and striking wooden altar are enough to warrant a good helping of "ooohs" and "aaaahs" from Catholics and non-Catholics alike. The appreciation continues for the basilica's light shows, which are set to music and make for an experience that's quite a bit more exciting than the usual Sunday service. ⏱ *30 min. 110 rue Notre-Dame ouest.* ☎ *514/842-2925. Admission for basilica C$4 adults, C$2 ages 7–17, free for those attending services. Light show C$10 adults, C$9 seniors, C$5 ages 7–17, free for kids ages 6 and under. Open Mon–Fri 8am–4:30pm, Sat 8am–4:15pm, Sun 12:30–4:15pm. Guided tours in English and French daily 9am–4pm. Call for light show times. Métro: Place d'Armes.*

Maple syrup is synonymous with the Laurentian forest outside Montréal,

Locals love to hang out at Vieux-Port on sunny days.

and you can shop for excellent maple syrups, spreads, and candles while you take a breather at 6 **Les Delices de l'Erable.** In addition to the usual cafe fare, this branch of a small chain of shop/cafes serves gelato. A plus: Curious customers can peer into the kitchen through a large window, tucked in the back of the cafe, and watch the cooks manipulate maple into its various forms. *84 rue St-Paul est.* ☎ *514/765-3456. Métro: Place d'Armes. $.*

The breathtaking interior of the Basilique Notre Dame.

7 ★★★ kids **Vieux-Port.** The city's Old Port catapulted Montréal's commercial and economic status over the last 200 years, but was a bit dreary until it got a face-lift in the early 1990s. Now, the converted waterfront, known as the Quays, is a playground for in-line skaters, cyclists, and couples out for a stroll. Bike rentals start at C$9.50 an hour (Conveyors Quay-Alexandra entrance; ☎ 514/289-9927). Quadricycles for couples and families are also available for C$4.35 to C$5 an hour (Jacques Cartier Quay; ☎ 514/849-9953). Anyone with sore feet can opt for the tram that scoots back and forth the length of the Old Port or for a relaxing daytime cruise on the St. Lawrence. By the end of the day most of the activity will have died down. Enjoy a meal in one of the restaurants, or head to the IMAX theater off Quai King Edward (p 37, bullet **6**) for a film. 🕐 *1 hr. Information Center: 333 rue de la Commune ouest (at Rue McGill).* ☎ *514/496-7678. www.quaysoftheoldport.com. Tram day pass C$7 adults, C$5.50 seniors, C$5.50 teenagers 13–17, C$5 children 12 and under, C$20 family. Métro: Champ-de-Mars, Place d'Armes, or Square Victoria.*

8 ★ **Hôtel de Ville.** The mayor of Montréal spends enough hours locked in his office in this impressive French Empire–style building that he probably only gets to enjoy the exterior's wonderfully lit details during his lunch break. If you arrive before it closes, visit the ornate Hall of Honour and marvel at the impressive French chandeliers and Italian marble. But it's after dark that the 19th-century city hall (restored after a fire in the early 1900s to resemble the Hôtel de Ville in Tours, France) is truly a sight. It's then that dramatic lighting drapes the Hôtel de Ville's exterior in soft hues, accentuating every nook and cranny of its

The impressive Hôtel de Ville, overlooking Place Jacque Cartier, is especially picturesque at night.

extraordinary architecture. Easily one of the most photogenic sites in Old Montréal. 🕐 *30 min. 275 rue Notre-Dame.* ☎ *514/872-3355. Free admission. Daily 8:30am–4:30pm. Métro: Champ-de-Mars.*

The Marché Bonsecours dominates the skyline of Vieux-Montréal. See p 59.

The Best **in Two Days**

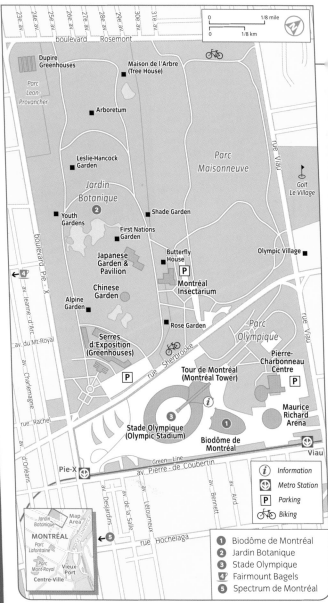

0	1/8 mile
0	1/8 km

boulevard Rosemont

Dupire Greenhouses

Maison de l'Arbre (Tree House)

Parc Leon-Provancher

Arboretum

Leslie-Hancock Garden

Jardin Botanique ❷

Parc Maisonneuve

rue Viau

Golf Le Village

Youth Gardens

Shade Garden

First Nations Garden

Japanese Garden & Pavilion

Butterfly House

P

Montréal Insectarium

Olympic Village

boulevard Pie-X

av. Jeanne-d'Arc

← ❹

Chinese Garden

Alpine Garden

av. du Mt-Royal

Rose Garden

Parc Olympique

rue Viau

av. Charlemagne

Serres d'Exposition (Greenhouses)

rue Sherbrooke

P

Tour de Montréal (Montréal Tower)

i

Pierre-Charbonneau Centre

P

rue Rachel

Stade Olympique (Olympic Stadium) ❸

Maurice Richard Arena

av. d'Orléans

Biodôme de Montréal ❶

Viau

Pie-X ◉

Green Line
av. Pierre - de - Coubertin

av. Desjardins

av. de-la-Salle

av. Létourneux

av. Bennett

av. Aird

i	Information
◉	Metro Station
P	Parking
🚲	Biking

Map Area

Jardin Botanique

MONTRÉAL

← ❺

Parc Lafontaine

Parc Mont-Royal

Vieux-Port

Centre-Ville

rue Hochelaga

❶	Biodôme de Montréal
❷	Jardin Botanique
❸	Stade Olympique
❹	Fairmount Bagels
❺	Spectrum de Montréal

Now that the big-name sights have been crossed off the list, it's time to stray from the downtown area. The northwest reaches of the city are home to one of the world's best and biggest gardens, and to Olympic Park—a financial folly built for the 1976 Summer Olympics that nevertheless gifted Montréal with the infrastructure for some medal-worthy attractions. START: **Viau Métro Station.**

Biodôme and Stade Olympique were both built for the 1976 Summer Olympics and are now two of the top attractions in the city.

① ★★★ **kids Biodôme de Montréal.** Few places in the world can boast having more than 4,000 creatures and 5,000 species of flora in four completely separate ecosystems under the same roof. But that's exactly the case at the one-of-a-kind Biodôme, originally built as the velodrome for the 1976 Olympic Summer Games. The eco-friendly attraction is home to four distinct biomes: the familiar Laurentian forest, a marine system modeled after the St. Lawrence river, a tropical rainforest, and a polar environment. Each biome is constructed so that most of the plants and animals (including many endangered species) found within are growing, crawling, or running in their respective environments. ⏱ *2 hr. 4777 av. Pierre-de-Coubertin (next to Olympic Stadium).* ☎ *514/ 868-3000. www.biodome.qc.ca. Admission C$13 adults, C$9.50 seniors and students, C$6.50 kids 5–17,* free for kids under 5. Discount combination tickets available for Jardin Botanique, Insectarium, Stade Olympique, and Biodôme. Daily 9am–5pm (until 6pm in late June, July–Aug). Closed most Mon Jan–Feb and Sept–Dec. Métro: Viau.

Penguins are just one of the many species of animal that call the Biodôme home.

Travel Tip

Be sure to take advantage of the free shuttle bus that stops at Stade Olympique, the Biodôme, and the Jardin Botanique. It's essential in summer, when the mercury can rise to blistering temps. Schedules are available at all of the participating attractions.

2 ★★ **Jardin Botanique.** It's time to stop and smell the flowers. Just over 75 years old, Montréal's sprawling 75-hectare (185-acre) Botanical Garden is home to 22,000 species of plants. Instead of using all that space for random flower arrangements and shrubbery sculptures, here you'll find individual greenhouses and cultural gardens (especially notable are the Chinese Garden—the largest outside of Asia—and the Japanese Garden) and the Insectarium (p. 36, bullet **2**), where kids will have a blast shrieking and giggling at the creepy, crawly displays. Covering the major sights here in less than 2 hours is an ambitious undertaking, so take advantage of the tram that runs around the entire garden—it's well worth the small fee. The Jardin Botanique, despite the city's frigid winters, is open year-round, and you'll always discover something blooming. ⌚ *1½ hr. 4101 rue Sherbrooke est.* ☎ *514/872-1400. www.ville.Montreal.qc.ca/jardin. Admission C$9.75–C$13 adults, C$7.25–C$9.50 seniors and students, C$4.75–C$6.50 ages 5–17, free for kids under 5. Combination tickets available for Jardin Botanique, Insectarium, Stade Olympique, and Biodôme. Daily 9am–5pm (until 6pm in summer, until 9pm mid-Sept to Oct). Closed Mon early Jan to mid-May. Métro: Pie-IX.*

Montréal's botanical gardens are among the largest and most beautiful in the world.

The Olympic Tower offers spectacular views of the city.

tickets available for Jardin Botanique, Insectarium, Stade Olympique, and Biodôme. Tour of stadium. Public swim sessions daily (call for exact schedule). Tower open mid-June to early Sept Mon noon–6pm, Tues–Thurs 10am–9pm, Fri–Sat 10am–11pm; early Sept to mid-Jan and mid-Feb to mid-June daily noon–6pm. Closed mid-Jan to mid-Feb. Métro: Pie-IX.

The Montréal version of the bagel is made quite differently than its more famous New York rival (smaller, denser and boiled in honeyed water before it's fired up in the oven). The distinctly textured version turned out by ☕ **Fairmount bagels** is well worth a trek. *74 Fairmount ouest. ☎ 514/272-0667. www.fairmount bagel.com. $.*

3 Stade Olympique. Compared to modern stadiums, The "Big O" is undeniably grotesque. Built for the 1976 Olympics, it became the home of Major League Baseball's expansion Montréal Expos, until they packed up and moved to Washington, D.C., in 2005. The stadium is now home to exhibitions, trade shows, and the occasional concert. An observation deck sits atop the slanted Olympic Tower (you ride a funicular to the top) on the stadium's roof and offers some of the best panoramas of the city. Visitors looking to cool off can dive off the platforms in the complex's natatorium or swim in its six pools. 🕐 *45 min. 4141 av. Pierre-de-Coubertin (bd. Pie IX). ☎ 514/252-4737. www.rio.gouv.qc.ca. Admission C$13 adults, C$10 seniors and students, and C$7 kids. Discount combination*

5 Spectrum de Montréal. A truly special way to top off your day is to unwind at a show in downtown's Spectrum de Montréal, a major blip on the city's cultural radar. This celebrated venue, housed in a converted movie theater, hosts everything from International Jazz Festival performances and local music groups to some of the biggest names in rock 'n' roll. People who've played here in the past include Miles Davis, Pavement, The Fugees, Massive Attack, and Peter Gabriel. And if you show up when the city's famous film festival is in full swing, you'll find the section of Rue St. Catherine around the Spectrum closed off to create a free open-air theater. For more details on the theater, see p 118. 🕐 *2 hr. 318 rue Ste-Catherine. ☎ 514/861-5851. www.spectrumdeMontréal.ca/spectrum. Métro: Place des Arts.*

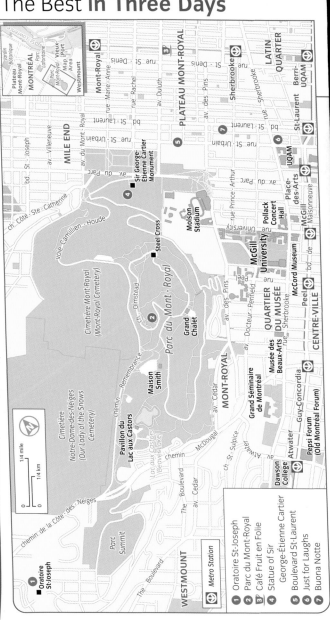

The Best **Full-Day Tours**

The Best **in Three Days**

MONTRÉAL

Jardin Botanique

Parc Lafontaine

Plateau Mont-Royal

Parc Mont-Royal Map Area

Vieux-Port

Westmount

- **1** Oratoire St-Joseph
- **2** Parc du Mont-Royal
- **3** Café Fruit en Folie
- **4** Statue of Sir George-Étienne Cartier
- **5** Boulevard St-Laurent
- **6** Just for Laughs
- **7** Buona Notte

Metro Station

WESTMOUNT

Parc Summit

Cimetière Notre-Dame-des-Neiges (Our Lady of the Snows Cemetery)

Cimetière Mont-Royal (Mont-Royal Cemetery)

Parc du Mont-Royal

MILE END

PLATEAU MONT-ROYAL

LATIN QUARTER

Mont-Royal

Sherbrooke

Sir George-Étienne Cartier Monument

Steel Cross

Grand Chalet

Maison Smith

Pavillon du Lac aux Castors

Molson Stadium

McGill University

Pollack Concert Hall

McCord Museum

QUARTIER DU MUSÉE

Musée des Beaux-Arts

Grand Séminaire de Montréal

MONT-ROYAL

CENTRE-VILLE

Dawson College

Pepsi Forum (Old Montréal Forum)

UQAM

Place-des-Arts

Guy-Concordia

Atwater

With two days of heavy sightseeing done, you deserve to take it easy and enjoy the more relaxing side of Montréal. People-watching and soaking up the outdoor spirit of the city are as rewarding experiences as visiting the city's museums and cultural institutions. On this third day of exploration, take advantage of the opportunity to see how the city got its name—and its reputation as the most vibrant metropolis in Canada. START: **Côtes-des-Neiges Métro station.**

Religious pilgrims flock to the Oratoire St-Joseph in search of miraculous healing.

1 ★ **Oratoire St-Joseph.** This enormous copper-domed structure is one of the most recognizable in Montréal, although you'll need to trek to the northern side of Mont-Royal to see it. The basilica, completed in 1967, honors the patron saint of Canada, St. Joseph. On the premises is a museum detailing the life of Brother André, a lay brother in the Holy Cross order and legendary healer, who first built a shrine to St. Joseph on this site in 1904. Many still visit Brother André's burial site on the basilica grounds in the hopes of a miracle healing. Others admire the gargantuan dome atop the Italian Renaissance building, listen to the 56-bell carillon (originally cast for the Eiffel Tower), or climb the 100 steps (some religious pilgrims do it on their knees!) leading to the highest point in the city to pray at the shrine. You can explore on your own, or you can take a 90-minute guided tour (in one of several languages) daily in summer and on weekends in fall.

🕐 *1 hr. 3800 Chemin Queen Mary (north side of Mont-Royal).* ☎ *514/ 733-8211. www.saint-joseph.org. Admission and tours are free, but donations are requested. Crypt open daily 6am–10:30pm; museum daily 10am–5pm. Tours 10am and 2pm daily June–Aug, Sat–Sun only, Sept– Oct. Métro: Côtes-des-Neiges.*

2 ★★ **Parc du Mont-Royal.** Renowned landscape architect Frederick Law Olmsted (1822–1903), after designing New York's Central Park, left his mark on Montréal by creating the Parc du Mont-Royal (Royal Mountain Park) in 1876. More hill than mountain, Mont-Royal, the 232m (761-ft.) peak for which the city is named, provides Montréalers with a slew of facilities for recreational activities. Hikers can trek

The view from the top of Mont-Royal is one of the best in the city.

through the miles of paths that snake through the park, sunbathers and Frisbee tossers can hang out near man-made Beaver Lake in summer, visitors in winter can opt for skiing or tobogganing on the mountain's slope, and shutterbugs can snap panoramic photos from the Chalet du Mont-Royal's terrace (at the crest of the hill) year-round. Before tackling Mont-Royal on your own, head to the park's information center, **Maison Smith,** 1260 chemin Remembrance, for specialized maps and/or books. For full details on the park's offerings, see p 49. ⏱ *2 hr. Entrance on av. des Pins and rue Peel.* ☎ *514/843-8240. www.lemontroyal.com. Park grounds open 24 hr.; information center Mon–Fri 9am–5pm, Sat–Sun 10am–6pm. Métro: Peel for the south side, Côtes-des-Neiges for the north.*

A relaxed walk in the Parc du Mont-Royal can quickly turn into a tiring one if you're running on empty. Refuel at the 3 **Café Fruit en Folie,** a popular breakfast nook in the Plateau. Traditional recipes are given a unique, fruity twist here, with amazing results. Each breakfast plate comes with enough fruit to

Statue of Sir George-Étienne Cartier.

satisfy your fiber needs for a week. It also serves American standards for lunch. *3817 rue St-Denis.* ☎ *514/ 840-9011. $$.*

❹ **Statue of Sir George–Étienne Cartier.** Just north of the park's gazebo, set on a large swath of grass on the eastern flank of the park, is the statue of Sir George-Étienne Cartier (1814–1873), a leading French-Canadian statesman known as the Father of Confederation. The best times to relax here are Sundays in the spring and summer when the statue sits in the center of an enormous percussion jam. During the event, dubbed "Tam Tams" by students and locals, the area around the statue fills with hundreds of sunbathers, hackey-sackers, jewelry vendors, LARPers (live-action role-playing), hippies and, most notably, bongo drummers. Mr. Cartier passively looks on as one main "conductor" leads a horde of pounding participants. If you have a set of bongos, congas, an empty plastic tub, or anything that makes a loud banging sound, you're more than qualified to join in the cacophony. ⏱ *1 hr. Av. du Parc (near av. Duluth).*

Musicians play at Montréal's world-famous International Jazz Festival.

5 ★★★ **Boulevard St-Laurent.** Also known as "The Main," St-Laurent continuously hums with off-beat boutiques and trendy restaurants packing the sidewalks with shoppers, students, and sightseers. Spend some time strolling, snacking, and people-watching your way up the boulevard. It becomes a 20-something's playground when the sun goes down—the dive bars and dance clubs that line the bustling street are immensely popular with the city's ubiquitous college undergrads. ***Tip:*** For one weekend in the spring, a long stretch of St-Laurent north of Rue Sherbrooke is closed off for what locals call "Main Madness," a massive street fair during which store owners and bartenders move their racks and tables out onto the asphalt. *Bd. St-Laurent, north of Rue Sherbrooke.* ⏱ *1½ hr. Métro: St-Laurent.*

The spectacular International Fireworks Competition is held each summer in Montréal.

City of Festivals

Few cities in North America can rival Montréal when it comes to celebrations lasting more than a couple of days. Throughout the year, the city is home to some of the biggest and most heralded festivals in the world. Attending one of them can make for a very memorable vacation. A small year-round sampling includes **Mutek** (electronica), **Francofolie** (French-language music), **Beer Tasting Festival, International Fireworks Competition, Montréal Bike Fest,** and **Image & Nation** (gay/lesbian film). The summer months are when the city hits full festival stride—the most renowned occurring within just weeks of each other. Most notably, there's the **International Jazz Festival** (June–July), **Juste Pour Rire Comedy Festival** (July), and **World Film Festival** (late Aug–early Sept). Booking a hotel room during one of these major events can be impossibly difficult, so make sure you try months in advance or you'll have to settle for some roadside motel in Vermont. For dates and more information on all of these shindigs, see "Festivals & Special Events," on p 144.

6 Just for Laughs. Boulevard St-Laurent, just below Rue Sherbrooke, becomes chuckle-central in the balmy month of July. The Juste Pour Rire Comedy Festival's main performance area also doubles as a venerable comedy museum. Gilbert Rozon founded this homage to comedy's legends in 1993, just as the festival was garnering great acclaim and popularity. Various exhibitions are held here throughout the year, with displays celebrating cartoonists, comedians, and magic and comedy histories. Call for ticket reservations ahead of time; the museum usually only allows groups into the permanent International Humour Hall of Fame Exhibition, but you may be able to gain admission if you call and convince them otherwise (and you should). In any event, you can always catch a show or concert in one of the spaces within the building. 🕐 1 hr. 2111 bd. St-Laurent. ☎ 514/845-4000. Tickets ☎ 514/845-5105. http://musee.hahaha.com. Admission C$9 adults, C$5 kids ages 4 to 11. Métro: St-Laurent.

7 Buona Notte. Finish off your day in Buona Notte, Montréal's glitziest restaurant. As you get to the corner of Boulevard St-Laurent

The Just Pour Rire Comedy Festival is held in several venues across the city, including the Just For Laughs comedy club.

and rue Milton, you'll trip over the expensive, pimped-out cars parked outside only to find more bodywork on the eerily beautiful people inside. If you can avert your eyes, a delicious meal here will momentarily distract you from the celebrities and models mingling and dining on *penne alla vodka*. 3518 bd. St-Laurent. ☎ 514/848-0644. Métro: St-Laurent. See p 91 for details on the restaurant. ●

The Buona Notte restaurant is where Montréal's beautiful people congregate for dinner and cocktails.

2 Best Special-Interest Tours

Cultural Montréal

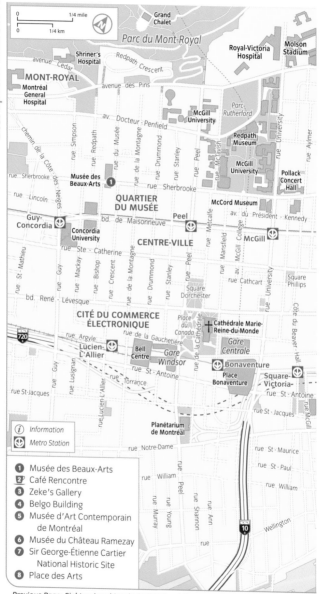

0   1/4 mile
0   1/4 km

Parc du Mont-Royal

Grand Chalet

Royal-Victoria Hospital

Molson Stadium

Shriner's Hospital

avenue Cedar

Redpath Crescent

MONT-ROYAL

Montréal General Hospital

avenue des Pins

chemin de la Côte-des-Neiges

av. Docteur - Penfield

McGill University

Parc Rutherford

Redpath Museum

McGill University

Pollack Concert Hall

rue Simpson

rue Redpath

rue du Musée

rue de la Montagne

rue Drummond

rue Stanley

rue Peel

rue McTavish

rue University

rue Aylmer

rue Sherbrooke

rue Lincoln

Musée des Beaux-Arts ❶

QUARTIER DU MUSÉE

rue Sherbrooke

McCord Museum

av. du Président - Kennedy

Guy-Concordia ◍

Concordia University

bd. de Maisonneuve

Peel ◍

Metcalfe

McGill College

McGill ◍

CENTRE-VILLE

rue Ste - Catherine

rue St-Mathieu

rue Guy

rue Mackay

rue Bishop

rue Crescent

rue de la Montagne

rue Drummond

rue Stanley

rue Peel

av. Cathcart

rue University

Square Phillips

bd. René - Lévesque

Square Dorchester

rue Cathcart

rue Mansfield

CITÉ DU COMMERCE ÉLECTRONIQUE

Place du Canada

Cathédrale Marie-Reine-du-Monde

Côte du Beaver - Hall

720

rue Argyle

rue de la Gauchetière

Lucien-L'Allier ◍

Bell Centre

Gare Windsor

Gare Centrale

rue Guy

rue Lusignan

rue St - Antoine

rue Torrance

Bonaventure ◍

Place Bonaventure

Square-Victoria- ◍

rue St - Antoine

rue St-Jacques

rue Lucien-L'Allier

rue St - Jacques

rue McGill

Planétarium de Montréal

rue Notre-Dame

rue St - Maurice

rue St - Paul

rue William

rue Peel

rue William

rue Murray

rue Young

rue Shannon

rue Ann

10

rue

Wellington

ⓘ Information

◍ Metro Station

❶ Musée des Beaux-Arts
❷ Café Rencontre
❸ Zeke's Gallery
❹ Belgo Building
❺ Musée d'Art Contemporain de Montréal
❻ Musée du Château Ramezay
❼ Sir George-Étienne Cartier National Historic Site
❽ Place des Arts

Previous Page: Sightseeing ships docked at the picturesque Vieux-Port.

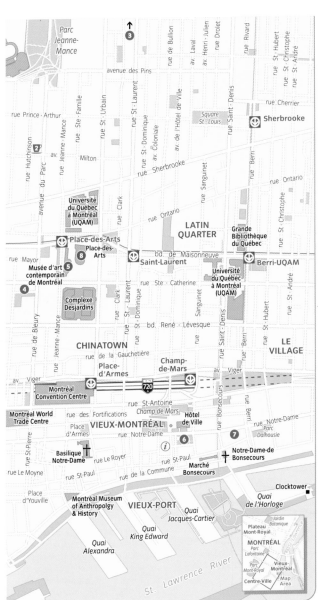

Y ou, too, would be throwing festivals every other week if you had a deep history and an amazing artistic tradition like Montréal's. With comprehensive museums, nurturing galleries and an unparalleled music community, the city stands alone as Canada's cultural mecca. This tour covers some of the city's most incredible institutions, allowing you to sample works painted by Renaissance masters, aural masterpieces by one of the world's most respected symphonies, and funky mixed-media displays from rising Canadian artists. START: **Métro: Peel or Guy-Concordia station.**

1 ★★★ Musée des Beaux-Arts. The best hunting ground for art hounds in Montréal is one of Canada's most comprehensive art repositories. For a more regional perspective, head to the museum's neoclassical Michal and Renata Hornstein Pavilion, where you'll find the museum's exceptional collection of Canadian art, including a number of outstanding landscapes by Canada's famed Group of Seven. If you prefer a wider range of styles, check out the ultramodern Moshe Safdie-designed Jean-Noël Desmarais Pavilion, which is home to the museum's wonderful collection of Old European masters, a number of decent Impressionist paintings (including an unusual still life by Renoir), and some good modern works by the likes of Picasso and Miró. ⏱ 1½ hr. See p 10, bullet **1**.

The Musée des Beaux-Arts is known primarily for its European and Canadian paintings, but also houses an excellent collection of sculpture.

A small Middle Eastern cafe, **2 Café Rencontre,** serves falafels, samosas, and various salads packed with enough herbs to clear your sinuses on a cold winter day. Grab a hot cup of coffee and watch the chess-playing regulars hunched over their boards, or strike up an enlightening conversation with one of the philosophy grad students hanging out in the back. *3500 av. du Parc.* ☎ *514/844-6133. No credit cards. $.*

3 Zeke's Gallery. Chris "Zeke" Hand ignored critics and conservative artists when he opened this contemporary gallery in 1998. Hand wanted to give nascent artists an alternative entry point into the artistic community. For the most part, he's succeeded, though describing this small three-room space as "alternative" might be an understatement. It's more kitschy apartment than museum (some stuff is more junk than art), with exhibits ranging from the cutting edge to the downright weird. The last time I visited, I almost got tangled up in a collection made up mainly of plastic construction netting. Strange materials aside, a smiling Zeke is always present to welcome visitors and show them around his mad museum. 🕐 30 min. 3955 bd. St-Laurent. ☎ 514/288-2233. http://zekesgallery.blogspot.com. Free admission. Open Sat–Thurs 4–8pm; to arrange earlier visits, call Zeke. Métro: St-Laurent.

❹ ★ **Belgo Building.** This brick-and-limestone building, completed in 1913, was originally part of the city's garment district but today is home to the studios of many young photographers, various artists, and dance schools. Much of the space is dedicated to such innovative galleries as **Thérèse Dion Art Contemporain** (www.theresedion.com) and **Optica** (www.optica.ca), which showcase contemporary paintings, photos, and sculptures. If you have time to explore one more, be sure to check out **Galerie René Blouin** (www.galierereneblouin.com), whose exhibitions rarely fail to impress. 🕐 1 hr. 372 rue Ste-Catherine ouest. No phone. Admission free to all galleries. Therese Dion open noon–6pm Tues–Sat; Optica open noon–5pm Tues–Sat; Galerie Rene Blouin open 10am–5:30pm Tues–Fri, 11am–5pm on Sat. Métro: Place-des-Arts.

Zeke's Gallery specializes in quirky art exhibits.

A sculpture at the innovative Thérèse Dion gallery.

❺ ★★ **Musée d'Art Contemporain de Montréal.** Defining anything from the 1940s and up as contemporary, this popular museum contains enough artwork from recent years (much of it thought provoking) to justify its name. The well-designed exhibit halls, all smartly arranged with photographs, canvases, and sculptures, never feel crowded even though the museum is one of the most visited cultural attractions in the city. The majority of the nearly 7,000-piece collection is by Québécois artists, including the largest group of works in the world by abstract painter Paul-Émile Borduas (1905–1960). You'll also find works by international artists and photographers (including Robert Mapplethorpe and Max Ernst) in a wide range of styles. Be sure to stop in at the museum's excellent boutique (p 11). 🕐 1½ hr. 185 rue Ste-Catherine ouest. ☎ 514/847-6226. www.macm.org. Admission C$8 adults, C$6 seniors, C$4 *students, free for kids under 12, C$16 for families; free admission Wed 6–9pm. Tues–Sun 11am–6pm (until 9pm Wed). Open Mon June 20–Sept 10. Métro: Place des Arts.*

⑥ ★ Musée du Château Ramezay.

Often overlooked by the tourist hordes, this small château—the first to be classified a historical monument in Quebec—dates back to 1705, when it was built by the colonial governor, Claude de Ramezay, as his official residence. Before it was converted into a historical museum in 1895, it served as a courthouse; as the headquarters of the American army (Ben Franklin slept here!), which invaded Montréal in 1775; and as Laval University's headquarters. Today you'll find a variety of antique tools, clothing, furniture (most from the late 18th- and early 19th-centuries), and other memorabilia on display. Don't miss the exhibits housed in the original

The Musée d'Art Contemporain is a sure bet for thought-provoking art.

cellar vaults, which depict re-creations of the everyday life of 18th-century Montréal, and the lovely herb garden behind the château. ⏱ 1 hr. 280 rue Notre-Dame est. ☎ 514/861-3708. www.chateau ramezay.qc.ca. Admission C$7.50 adults, C$6 seniors, C$5 students, C$4 children 5–17, free for children under 5. Museum and garden open daily 10am–6pm (June 1–mid-Oct). Museum open Tues–Sun 10am–4:30pm (mid-Oct–May 31). Métro: Champ-de-Mars.

Recreations of 18th-century life in Montréal are the prime reason to visit the Musée du Château Ramezay.

⑦ ★ Sir George-Étienne Cartier National Historic Site of Canada.

This worthwhile stop often flies under the tourist radar but deserves more attention. Parks Canada has beautifully restored the two adjoining residences that once housed the family of Sir George-Étienne Cartier (1814–1873), a renowned French-Canadian statesman known as the "Father of Confederation." The first two rooms open to visitors give you an admirable crash course in the history of Canadian politics with a few multimedia displays, but the museum's true gems are the detailed reconstructions of the family living quarters. These show what life was like for upper-class Montréalers, not just the Cartiers, in the late 19th century. Audio consoles spit out don't-miss vocal performances in both French and English by

actors and actresses playing the parts of the chambermaid and other members of the house staff. The historic site also stages live, interactive theatrical performances featuring the Cartier family and their servants throughout the year (call in advance for the current schedule). ◷ *1 hr. 458 Notre-Dame est.* ☎ *514/283-2282 or 888/773-8888. www.pc.gc. ca/cartier. Admission to museum: C$4 adults, C$3.50 seniors, C$2 children, C$10 family/group. Heritage Presentation (interactive theater): C$6.25 adults, C$5.50 seniors, C$4.25 children, C$16 family/group. Open daily 10am–6pm June–Sept, Wed–Sun 10am–5pm Apr–May and Sept–Dec. Métro: Champs-de-Mars.*

8 ★★ **Place des Arts.** Don your finest eveningwear and settle in for a night of refined entertainment. The only cultural complex of its kind in Canada, Place des Arts is home to five concert halls and theaters (ranging in size from large to intimate), which host Montréal's symphony

One of several re-created historic interiors at the Sir George-Étienne Cartier National Historic Site of Canada.

orchestra, operas, and other theatrical performances. During certain festivals and events, the center's outdoor plaza is sometimes used as an open-air theatre, a fireworks viewing area and, if you're lucky, for Cirque du Soleil performances. ◷ *1hr. 175 rue Ste-Catherine ouest.* ☎ *514/842-2112 (Salle Wilfrid-Pelletier). www.pda.qc.ca. Hours and prices vary; check the website for a current schedule, and see chapter 8 for information on the center's various theaters and concert halls. Métro: Place des Arts.*

Place des Arts—Canada's top cultural complex.

Romantic Montréal

MONTRÉAL
Longueuil
Lachine
Lasalle
La Prairie
St Laurent
Ch. de la Côte-Ste-Catherine

MILE END
Rosemont
Parc Père-Marquette
Parc Sir-Wilfrid-Laurier
rue St - Denis
bd. St - Laurent
av. Laurier
bd. St - Joseph
Laurier
PLATEAU MONT-ROYAL ❷
Papineau
av. du Mont - Royal
Mont-Royal
Parc du Mont-Royal
Parc Jeanne-Mance
Monument Sir-George-Étienne Cartier
Steel Cross
rue Rachel
av. Denis
Duluth
Parc Lafontaine ❸
av. des Pins
Sherbrooke
Sherbrooke
Ontario
Papineau
McGill University
McCord Museum
rue University
Place-des-Arts
LATIN QUARTER
Berri-UQAM
LE VILLAGE
Papineau
av.
❼
St - Laurent
rue Amherst
Peel
McGill
St-Laurent ❺
bd. de Maisonneuve
Beaudry
CENTRE-VILLE
rue Ste - Catherine
CHINATOWN
INTERNATIONAL QUARTER
Champ-de-Mars
bd. René - Lévesque
Bonaventure
Square-Victoria
❹ 720
Place-d'Armes
rue St - Antoine
rue Notre - Dame
Montréal Convention Centre
VIEUX-MONTRÉAL ❻
10
VIEUX-PORT
CITÉ DU MULTIMEDIA
Île Sainte-Hélène
Parc Jean-Drapeau
Biosphere
Jean-Drapeau
Pont de la Concorde
Île Notre-Dame

0   1/4 mile
0   1/4 km

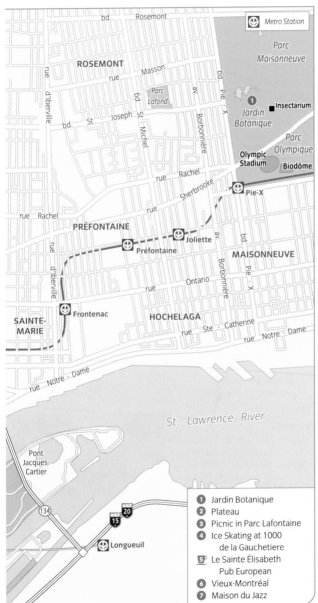

Metro Station

bd. Rosemont

Parc
Maisonneuve

ROSEMONT

rue Masson

Parc
Lafond

bd. St - Joseph

1 Jardin
Botanique

■ Insectarium

Parc
Olympique

Olympic
Stadium

Biodôme

rue Rachel

Sherbrooke

Pie-X

rue Rachel

PRÉFONTAINE

Préfontaine

Joliette

MAISONNEUVE

Ontario

Frontenac

HOCHELAGA

rue Ste - Catherine

**SAINTE-
MARIE**

rue Notre - Dame

rue Notre - Dame

St. Lawrence River

Pont
Jacques-
Cartier

134

20
15

Longueuil

1 Jardin Botanique
2 Plateau
3 Picnic in Parc Lafontaine
4 Ice Skating at 1000
de la Gauchetiere
5 Le Sainte Élisabeth
Pub European
6 Vieux-Montréal
7 Maison du Jazz

Whether they're falling in love with the city or with each other, couples can depend on Montréal for little weekend getaways or charming vacations. An endless supply of picturesque neighborhoods and cozy eateries make it one of the most captivating cities in North America. START: **Métro: Pie-IX.**

For a romantic outdoor experience, you can't do much better than the Jardin Botanique.

❶ ★★ **Jardin Botanique.** You'll be hard pressed to find an area within the city's botanical gardens that isn't conducive to cuddling. For the ultimate in ambience, find a spot within the complex's themed gardens. The Japanese Garden, in particular, has an extremely relaxing Zen garden, a tearoom, and an art gallery where you can show off your cultural savvy to your date. 🕐 1½ hr. See p 16, bullet ❷.

❷ **Plateau.** Whether its tree-lined streets are littered with gold, orange, and scarlet leaves in the fall, or fresh snow in the winter, this area is perfect for any couple looking for a quiet, leisurely stroll. Grab a souvenir or cup of coffee at one of the many boutiques and cafes on St-Denis. Or head down the delightful tree-lined avenue Duluth, between St-Denis and St-Laurent, which is lined with a slew of romantic restaurants that offer intimate dining and feature international cuisine ranging from Japanese to Portuguese to Vietnamese. 🕐 1 hr. Area bordered by Blvd. St-Laurent to Rue Papineau and Rue Sherbrooke to Rue Laurier. Métro: Mont-Royal.

❸ ★ **Picnic in Parc Lafontaine.** Pack up some gourmet cheeses and a few baguettes (a good place to get them is Premiere Moisson, p. 97) for a tranquil picnic in the Plateau's gorgeous green space. Couples can snuggle up on a patch of grass alongside the scenic ponds on the quaint English (west) half of the park and then take a stroll through the dreamy garden paths in the distinct French (east) side. The park's a microcosm of Montréal, from its bilingual nature to its laid-back atmosphere to its mesmerizing beauty. 🕐 1½ hr. Rue Sherbrooke & av. du Parc Lafontaine. Métro: Sherbrooke.

❹ ★ **Ice Skating at 1000 de la Gauchetiere.** Escape the city's stifling heat or freezing cold at this year-round Underground City rink. Oddly shaped, with two large

The Plateau is one of Montréal's most picturesque and romantic neighborhoods.

A ride through Old Montréal in a hired horse-drawn carriage is a very popular activity for couples.

columns stuck in the middle, the sheltered and cozy rink is surrounded by plenty of eateries and cafes if you get hungry. Even if you don't know the difference between a triple-salchow and a snowplow, you'll have a fun time holding hands, falling over each other, and laughing as you circle the atrium. 🕐 *1 hr. 1000 rue de la Gauchetiere ouest.* ☎ *514/395–0555. www.le1000.com. Admission: C$5.50 adults, C$3.50 children 12 and under, C$4.50 seniors, C$5 skate rentals, C$2 locker rental. Open Tues–Fri, Sun 11:30am– 6pm, Sat 11:30am–10pm. Métro: Bonaventure.*

Though the surrounding neighborhood isn't the most glamorous, the dramatically lit interiors and magnificent terrace at 5 ★ **Le Sainte Élisabeth Pub European**, make a quick drink here a wonderfully romantic experience. Sip a glass of port or sample their Ste-Elisabeth beer, a tasty ale brewed in-house. See p. 107. *1412 rue St-Elisabeth.* ☎ *514/286-4302. www.ste-elisabeth.com.*

6 ★★★ **Vieux-Montréal.** Much of Montréal's charm and elegance can be traced here. The old-world feel of Old Montréal's narrow, 18th-century streets and the striking architecture of the buildings found south of rue St-Antoine is where this dynamic city gets most of its character. It's also home to some very romantic experiences. Soak up atmosphere at the bustling Place Jacques Cartier, stroll the long walkways along Vieux-Port, or stop in at one of the cafes on the cobblestone streets that snake through Vieux-Montréal. For the ultimate postcard moment, consider hiring a caléche (☎ 514/934-6105). These horse-drawn carriages may be corny and expensive (up to C$60–C$75 for an hour's ride), but they rarely disappoint the lovebirds who jump in them. Afterwards, to truly pamper your significant other, be sure to book a room in one of the B&B's in the area. 🕐 *1½ hr. For accommodations options in Vieux-Montréal, see chapter 9. Caléche pick-up points at Square Dorchester, Place Jacques Cartier, and Place d'Armes (just in front of the basilica). Métro: Champ de Mars, Place d'Armes.*

7 ★ **Maison du Jazz.** A city landmark, House of Jazz started life as Biddles, named after local jazz legend Charlie Biddle. When Biddle died in 2003, the club/restaurant got a name change, but it is still the city's premiere spot for jazz, featuring different performers almost every night. The food is as fine as the music: Dine on delicious steaks or salmon, accompanied by excellent wine, at candle-lit tables. The club's live music is a perfect accompaniment to a romantic meal. 🕐 *1½ hr. 2060 rue Aylmer.* ☎ *514/842-8656. www.houseofjazz.ca. Open Mon–Wed 11:30–12:30am, Thurs 11:30–1:30am, Fri 11:30–2:30am, Sat 6pm–2:30am, Sun 6pm–12:30am. Métro: McGill.*

Montréal with Kids

MONTRÉAL
Longueuil
Lachine
Lasalle
La Prairie

ch. de la Côte-Ste-Catherine

MILE END

Rosemont

Parc Père-Marquette

St - Laurent

rue St - Denis

av. Laurier

bd. St - Joseph

Laurier

PLATEAU MONT-ROYAL

Parc Sir-Wilfrid-Laurier

Papineau

Parc du Mont-Royal

Parc Jeanne-Mance

av. du

Steel Cross

Monument Sir-George-Étienne Cartier

av. du Mont - Royal

Mont-Royal

rue Rachel

av. Duluth

Parc Lafontaine

Papineau

av. des Pins

St - Denis

av. des Pins

rue

Sherbrooke

Sherbrooke

McGill University

rue University

rue

St - Laurent

bd.

rue

LATIN QUARTER

Amherst

Ontario

McCord Museum

Place-des-Arts

St-Laurent

Berri-UQAM

LE VILLAGE

Papineau

av.

Peel

McGill

bd. de Maisonneuve

Beaudry

CENTRE-VILLE

rue Ste - Catherine

CHINATOWN

bd. René - Lévesque

INTERNATIONAL QUARTER

Champ-de-Mars

Bonaventure

Square-Victoria

Montréal Convention Centre

Place-d'Armes

rue St - Antoine

rue Notre - Dame

720

VIEUX-MONTRÉAL

10

CITÉ DU MULTIMEDIA

VIEUX-PORT

Île Sainte-Hélène

Parc Jean-Drapeau

Biosphere

Jean-Drapeau

Pont de la Concorde

Île Notre-Dame

0   1/4 mile
0   1/4 km

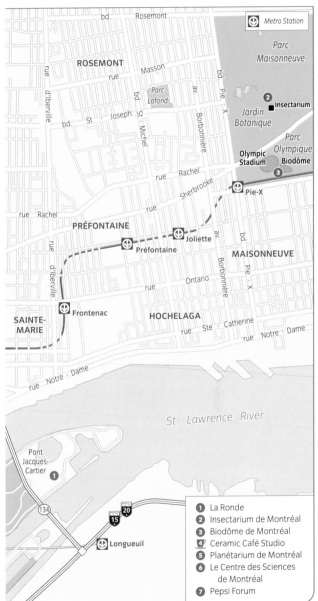

⊕ *Metro Station*

1. La Ronde
2. Insectarium de Montréal
3. Biodôme de Montréal
4. Ceramic Café Studio
5. Planétarium de Montréal
6. Le Centre des Sciences de Montréal
7. Pepsi Forum

At first glance, Montréal might seem more like a playground for adults than children. That perception couldn't be farther far from the truth. A good number of the city's museums and attractions tailor many of their exhibits and activities to the city's tiniest sightseers, and parents are sure to hear hours of giddy shrieks and astonished gasps when they hit the spots below. START: **Métro: Jean-Drapeau, then bus 167 to La Ronde.**

1 La Ronde. Though many of the 37 rides at this Six Flags–owned venture—Montréal's only amusement park—will test thrill seekers, little ones and less-adventuresome kids will find plenty of other fun options, including various multimedia extravaganzas and a slew of cutesy, slow rides. Older kids and teens (and fearless parents) should head for the extreme monstrosities, which include the 60mph (97kmph) Le Cobra coaster; and Le Vampire, a suspended coaster that does five loops at 50mph (80kmph). ⏱ *2 hr. 22 chemin Macdonald (Île Ste-Hélène).* ☎ *514/397-2000. www. laronde.com. Open daily late May to mid-June 10am–8pm, mid-June to late Aug 10am–10:30pm, Sept–Oct limited hours (see site or call). Admission: C$36 for those 54 in. and taller, C$24 for those under 54 in., free for kids under 3. Season passes available. Métro: Jean-Drapeau (then bus 167).*

2 ★★ Insectarium de Montréal. More than 3,000 species of creepy critters (either mounted, flying, or crawling in enclosed displays) call this two-story museum home. Kids especially adore the mounted butterflies and the live displays of scorpions, tarantulas, crickets, cockroaches, and praying mantises. If you're lucky (or unlucky, depending on your appetite) and happen to visit in the months of November and December, you can take part in the museum's **Insect Tasting,** where appointed experts in the field of bug cuisine fry up, bake, sauté and candy all sorts of six-legged creatures. ⏱ *1½ hr. 4581 rue Sherbrooke est.* ☎ *514/872-1400. www2.ville.Montréal.qc.ca/ insectarium. Open early Jan to mid-May 9am–5pm, mid-May to early Sept 9am–6pm, early Sept to Oct 9am–9pm, Nov to late Dec 9am–5pm. Admission to both Insectarium and Jardin Botanique: C$9.75–C$13 adults, C$4.75–C$6.50 children ages 5 through 17, C$7.25–C$9.50 students and seniors 65 and over, free for children under 5. Métro: Pie-IX or Viau.*

3 ★★★ Biodôme de Montréal. Of the four ecosystems (all with their appropriate temperatures, flora, and fauna) re-created in this unusual attraction, the polar and rainforest environments are the biggest hits with young kids—penguins and macaws apparently having the innate ability to mesmerize children for hours. Once they've gotten tired of watching the animals, little ones can try out Naturalia, a game room just for kids. Older children and teens usually find

This mantis is just one of the many creepies and crawlies you'll encounter at the Insectarium de Montréal.

all of the exhibits—and their wide range of animals, which include endangered species—fascinating. ⏱ 1½ hr. See p. 15, bullet ❶.

Unless you want funky tasting icing, you and your kids are better off devouring a yummy slice of cake **before** you get your hands messy with the ceramic painting at the ❹**Ceramic Café Studio.** For C$6 to C$8 an hour for adults, C$4 to C$6 an hour for kids, you get all the tools and supplies needed to decorate a piece of ceramic dishware (a cool souvenir). *4201B, rue St-Denis.* ☎ *514/848-1119. $–$$.*

❺ ★ **Planétarium de Montréal.** Young kids may fall asleep as they lean back and watch this planetarium's illuminations of the night sky, but older children will be intrigued by the exciting light shows and multimedia displays. The 20m (66-ft.) dome is modest as far as planetariums go, but its presentations (staged alternatively in French and English) are still impressive and informative, and the downtown location is very convenient. A special, worthwhile holiday show is screened in December and early January. ⏱ *1 hr. 1000 rue St-Jacques.* ☎ *514/872-4530. www.planetarium. Montréal.qc.ca. Call for current opening times and film schedules. Closed Christmas and New Year's Day. Admission C$8 adults, C$4 children 5–17, C$6 seniors and students, free for children under 5. Métro: Bonaventure.*

❻ ★ **Le Centre des Sciences de Montréal.** This ambitious and highly interactive science museum is filled with intriguing exhibits that enlighten visitors on a wide range of topics, from biology to telecommunications. The biggest draw for kids is the center's IMAX theater, where

The Planétarium de Montréal screens impressive light shows that usually enthrall older kids.

an enormous screen and booming speakers bombard children with vivid images of furry animals, bouncing molecules, hulking machines, and other science-related subjects. ⏱ *1½ hr. Quai King Edward (Vieux-Port).* ☎ *514/496-4724 or* ☎ *877/496-4724. www. Montréalsciencecentre.com. Open Sept 5–June 18 Mon–Fri 8:30am–3:30pm and Sat–Sun 10am–5pm; June 19–Sept 4, Mon–Fri 9am–5pm, Sat–Sun 10am–5pm. Call for IMAX theater schedule or check the website. Admission (various movie/exhibition combinations): C$10–C$22 adult, C$9–C$20 teenagers 13–17 and seniors (60+), C$7–C$18 children 4–12, C$30–C$60 families (2 adults & 2 kids or 1 adult & 3 kids).*

❼ **Pepsi Forum.** It was a sad day for Montréalers and hockey purists when the Montréal Canadiens moved from their legendary home, the Forum, to their current digs in the Bell Centre. The Forum has since been transformed into this giant shopping complex and entertainment center. The video games and bowling alley at Legendes du Forum, and the enormous AMC Forum movie theater, are just some of the kid-friendly places where families can unwind. ⏱ *1 hr. 2313 rue Ste-Catherine ouest.* ☎ *514/932-0000. Most shops open 11am–6pm; attraction hours vary, call for details. Métro: Atwater.*

Gastronomic Montréal

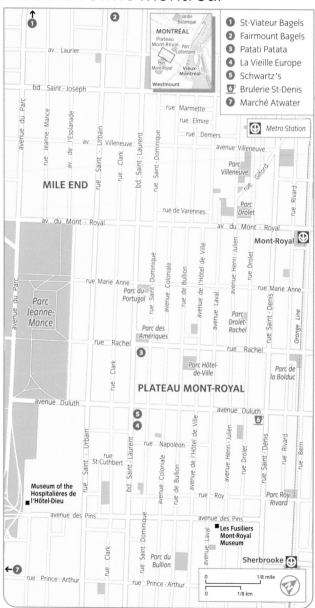

1 St-Viateur Bagels
2 Fairmount Bagels
3 Patati Patata
4 La Vieille Europe
5 Schwartz's
6 Brulerie St-Denis
7 Marché Atwater

Despite the prevalence of French and American influences on the local cuisine, the city's international flavor permeates the kitchens of its incredible restaurants and the shelves of its excellent gourmet groceries and markets, ultimately resulting in the creation of many foodstuffs that have become inextricably linked with Montréal. On this tour you get to sample the treats that have filled locals with a huge amount of pride—and an even bigger amount of calories. START: **Métro: Jean-Talon.**

Fairmount Bagels serves up more than 20 varieties of Montreal's most renowned baked goods every day.

❶ ★★ **St-Viateur Bagels.** Montréal's bagels' unique texture and delicious, honey-tinged flavor warrant not one, but a pair of entries on this tour—the two giants who battle it out every year for the title of "Best Bagel in the City." In recent years, locals have been partial to the offerings baked in the wood-burning ovens at St-Viateur. You can be the ultimate arbiter of quality for the crusty foodstuff by ordering a couple for the road. ⏱ *30 min. 263 St-Viateur ouest.* ☎ *514/ 276-8044. www.st viateurbagel.com. Open 24 hr. daily. Métro: Mont-Royal.*

❷ ★ **Fairmount Bagels.** It might play second fiddle to

St-Viateur, but Fairmount's doughy discs are worth the extra walk and added bagel bulk in your stomach. Sample one of the 20 wood-fired varieties, which range from plain to pesto and black olive to chocolate chip. ⏱ *30 min. 74 Fairmount ouest.* ☎ *514/272–0667. www.fairmount-bagel.com. Open 24 hr. daily. Métro: Laurier.*

❸ **Patati Patata.** It's hard to screw up melted cheese, gravy, and French fries, but it's also tough to create a version of *poutine* that stands out from the rest. Patati Patata accomplishes this with a perfect combination of cheese curds, fresh potatoes, and thick gravy. They even offer a "veggie poutine" that's still pretty unhealthy, so work off the impending artery clog with a brisk walk after you indulge. ⏱ *30 min. 4177 bd. St-Laurent.* ☎ *514/844–0216. Open Mon–Fri 8am–11pm, Sat–Sun 11am–11pm. Métro: Mont-Royal.*

❹ ★ **La Vieille Europe.** A whiff of practically every imaginable culinary scent will leave your salivary glands pumping and your stomach growling the second you enter this veritable warehouse of edibles. All sorts of savory meats, international cheeses (more than 300 varieties!), and gourmet condiments wait for patrons to assemble them into the

Poutine—french fries with cheese and gravy—is arguably the city's favorite fast food.

Marché Atwater, Montreal's best public market sells a mouthwatering array of fresh produce and other delicacies.

mother of all sandwiches. Before you do, get a caffeine fix by breathing in the coffee fumes from the huge, open bean-roaster in the back. 🕐 *30 min. 3855 bd. St-Laurent.* ☎ *514/842-5773. Open Mon–Wed 7:30am–6pm, Thurs–Fri 7:30am–9pm, Sat 7:30am–5pm, Sun 9am–5pm. Métro: Mont-Royal.*

5 ★★★ Schwartz's. There's a reason celebrities battle Schwartz's crowds and risk exposure to come to this cramped diner-style restaurant: The wonderfully sinful and perfectly seasoned slices of smoked meat are exponentially better than any sandwich meat you'll find in any other deli. Aged to perfection, the red-brown meat shavings are served in stacks or already in sandwich form. You'll sit shoulder-to-shoulder with other wild-eyed patrons, but

they'll soon be forgotten as you sink your teeth into layers of tasty rye and smoked meat. For the complete experience, wash down your sandwich with a chunk of dill pickle and a swig of Cott's black cherry cola. 🕐 *1 hr. See p. 98.*

What better way to aid the digestion than to gulp down some of the city's best java. Follow the smell of coffee beans on St. Denis to **6 Brulerie St-Denis.** The Canadian chains that try to compete with this coffee powerhouse can't hold a candle to the shop's rich brews. *3965 rue St-Denis.* ☎ *514/286-9158. $.*

7 ★★ Marché Atwater. If you still haven't found that one particular cheese or meat you're craving, chances are you'll find it at Marché Atwater. Perhaps the city's best public market, it's home to a plethora of vendors selling different breads, cheeses, meats, wines, and a motley assortment of other foods. 🕐 *1 hr. 138 rue Atwater. Open Mon–Wed 8am–6pm, Thurs 8am–8pm, Fri 8am–9pm, Sat–Sun 8am–5pm. Métro: Lionel-Groulx.* ●

A Tasty Mess

Though they're both essentially French fries with gravy and cheese on top, don't ever make the mistake of equating poutine with American "disco fries." Québécois will be quick to point out that the beauty of their beloved snack lies in the cheese. Real poutine uses cheese curds that don't melt completely into the mix while disco fries are usually just topped with shredded mozzarella. Legend has it that the dish's name originated in the 1950s, when restaurateur Fernand LaChance received a request from a customer for French fries and cheese in a bag. He then responded, *"Ca va faire une maudite poutine!"* Roughly translated: "That's going to make a damn mess." A mess it may have been, but it was also a bona fide culinary hit, made even more so when gravy was tacked on to the recipe a few years later. Today poutine is a fixture on the Quebec dining scene, and a must-try when you're in town.

Downtown Montréal

0   1/8 mile
0   1/8 km

Redpath Museum

rue Redpath

rue du Musée

rue de la Montagne

rue Drummond

rue Stanley

rue Peel

rue McTavish

1

Musée des Beaux-Arts

QUARTIER DU MUSÉE

rue Sherbrooke

Montreal Decorative Arts Museum

Guy-Concordia

Green Line

Peel

bd. de Maisonneuve

Concordia University

2

CENTRE-VILLE

rue Metcalfe

rue Mansfield

av. McGill College

rue Sainte - Catherine

3

rue Bishop

rue Crescent

rue de la Montagne

rue Drummond

rue Stanley

rue Peel

rue Cathcart

bd. René - Lévesque

Square Dorchester

rue Lucien-L'Allier

CITÉ DU COMMERCE ÉLECTRONIQUE

Place du Canada

Cathédrale Marie-Reine-du-Monde

✝

14

Lucien-L'Allier

rue de la Gauchetière

Orange Line

Gare Centrale

Bell Centre

Gare Windsor

rue Peel

rue de la Cathédrale

rue de la Gauchetière

Bonaventure

Place Bonaventure

rue Saint-Antoine

rue de la Montagne

Torrance

rue Saint-Jacques

Planétarium de Montréal

Metro Station

Previous page: The Illuminated Crowd, a sculpture set just in front of the Banque National de Paris tower in Downtown Montréal.

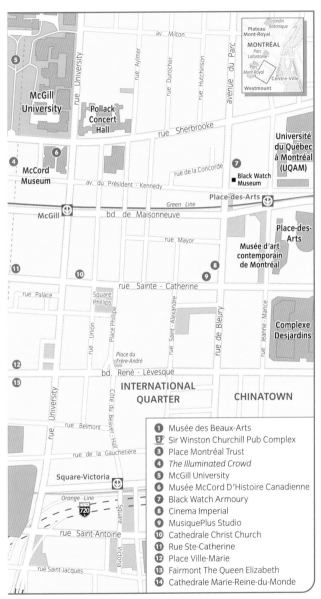

1 Musée des Beaux-Arts
2 Sir Winston Churchill Pub Complex
3 Place Montréal Trust
4 *The Illuminated Crowd*
5 McGill University
6 Musée McCord D'Histoire Canadienne
7 Black Watch Armoury
8 Cinema Imperial
9 MusiquePlus Studio
10 Cathedrale Christ Church
11 Rue Ste-Catherine
12 Place Ville-Marie
13 Fairmont The Queen Elizabeth
14 Cathedrale Marie-Reine-du-Monde

The buildings in Montréal's 20th-century downtown core aren't as densely packed as in other major cities in North America, and you could probably navigate the area's streets in a given afternoon, but Montréal's downtown is deceptively large. There are countless shops, museums, and attractions that could easily take a week to explore, so here are some that shouldn't take more than a day and that you shouldn't miss. START: **Métro: Peel or Guy Concordia Station.**

1 ★★★ **Musée des Beaux-Arts.** Canada's oldest and Montréal's finest museum encompasses two buildings: the modern Jean-Noel Desmarais Pavilion, built in 1991 to give the museum more room to showcase its immense collection; and the original Beaux Arts building (1912). The two buildings—both built of Vermont marble—are set directly across the street from each other, and are connected via an underground walkway that doubles as an art gallery. 🕐 *2 hr. See p 10, bullet* **1**.

Rue Crescent is loaded with cafes and snack spots that are fine for a quick bite. One good choice is **2** the **Sir Winston Churchill Pub Complex,** which serves light fare in its often-packed pub and at street-side tables that offer great people-watching. *1459 rue Crescent.* ☎ *514/288-0623. $.*

3 **Place Montréal Trust.** A gateway to the Underground City, centrally located at a very busy pedestrian intersection, this five-level mall usually bustles with action from morning to night (it averages 12 million visitors a year). Browse its many shops or check out its atrium, whose water fountain has the highest spout in North America. On warm days, you'll usually spot a saxophone busker belting out tunes in front of the popular shopping complex's Indigo bookshop. *1500 av. McGill College.* ☎ *514/843-8000. www.placemontrealtrust.com.*

The original building of the Musée des Beaux-Arts is home to its collection of decorative and Canadian art, among other works.

4 ★ *The Illuminated Crowd.* Set in front of the Banque National de Paris tower, this eggnog-colored work (1985), by English sculptor Raymond Mason, captures the detailed facial expressions of just over a dozen people in polyester resin. The faces represent a slew of emotional states, including hope, irritation, fear, death and, of course, illumination. Many find the piece evocative and exhilarating, but some think it a tad sentimental. *1981 av. McGill College.*

5 **McGill University.** The 32-hectare (80-acre) campus of Canada's most prestigious university cuts a lovely swath of green through downtown's urban core. Take a seat on the "Steps to Nowhere" (immediately on

your right as you pass through the stone Roddick Gates on rue Sherbrooke) to watch students frantically get to their classes. Or turn to your left as you enter and check out the large stone that marks the site of the Iroquois Hochelaga settlement that existed here before the arrival of the Europeans. Guided historical tours of the campus (which opened for classes in 1829), conducted by knowledgeable grad students, are offered by the school's Welcome Centre by prior arrangement only. *Main entrance on Rue Sherbrooke and Av. McGill College. www.mcgill.ca. To arrange a tour, e-mail your request to welcome@McGill.ca at least a week in advance. See p 11, bullet* ❸.

This grouse-shaped feast dish is just one of the many Canadian artifacts displayed at the Musée McCord D'Histoire Canadienne.

❻ ★★ **Musée McCord D'Histoire Canadienne.** The bulk of the approximately 1.4 million items on display at this private museum of Canadian history reside in the impressive Notman Photograph Archive. The rest of the collection consists of intriguing and informative displays made up of manuscripts, tools, clothing, furniture, jewelry, and other artifacts from Canada's history (18th–20th century). The exhibitions here are usually expertly curated and worthwhile. ⏱ *1½ hr. 690 rue Sherbrooke ouest.* ☎ *514/398-7100. www.mccordmuseum.qc.ca. Open Tues–Fri 10am–6pm, Sat–Sun 10am–5pm. Open Mon 10am–5pm on holiday weekends and during summer. Admission C$10 adults, C$7.50 seniors (65+), C$5.50 students, C$3 children 6–12, free for kids under 5, C$20 families; free admission 1st Sat of each month (10am–noon only).*

The Place Montréal Trust mall is one of the many retail developments that make up Montréal's famous Underground City.

❼ **Black Watch Armoury.** Canada's oldest Highland regiment, the Black Watch, originated in 1862, when six Scottish chieftains in Montréal responded to the Canadian government's call for a militia to patrol the border between Canada and the U.S. Now a regular part of the Canadian military, the Black Watch lives, trains, and practices their bagpipes in their castle-like headquarters. On some mornings, the sounds of bagpipes and drums can be heard emanating from the austere building as the regiment practices for the parade performances their Pipe & Drum Corps often give throughout the year (check the website for an up-to-date performance schedule). *2067 rue de Bleury. www.blackwatchcanada.com.*

❽ ★ **Cinema Imperial.** Montréal's oldest operating movie house, this historic one in Italian Renaissance style opened in 1913 as a vaudeville theater but was quickly adapted for film. It was donated to the World Film Festival in 1995, but closed for 2 years in 2001 for a massive and much-needed renovation. Today the city's only single-screen theater has a rather bland modern exterior, but its lush gold and red interiors have helped it maintain its regal character. *1430 rue de Bleury. See p 119.*

⑨ **MusiquePlus Studio.** Taking a page right out of MTV's playbook, Quebec's francophone music channel tapes their shows in a building that allows pedestrians to peep inside. Floor-to-ceiling windows allow shrieking teen fans to profess their love to whoever is visiting the studios on any given day. When there's no Quebec heartthrob or American pop-sensation in attendance, passersby can usually catch a glimpse of one of the channel's quirky veejays counting down the day's music videos. *Northwest corner of Rue de Bleury and Rue Ste-Catherine.*

⑩ **Cathedrale Christ Church.** Completed in 1859, this Anglican church was built of limestone in the Gothic style, though in 1927 a fault in the tower forced the church to replace the stone version with a

The Anglican Cathedrale Christ Church, set in the heart of downtown Montréal.

Rue Ste-Catherine is one the city's prime thoroughfares for shopping.

less-weighty aluminum one. Take a minute to relax in its lovely garden, modeled on a medieval European cloister, and you might notice that the ground-floor windows of the adjacent office building match the shape of the church's stained glass windows. Both the skyscraper and the shopping complex beneath the cathedral (Promenades de la Cathédrale) are owned by the church. A small exhibit in the Promenades de la Cathédrale illustrates the difficult building process—the church literally stood on an island of support columns as the retail complex was built under it—with photographs and sketches. ⏱ *30 min. 1444 av. Union (entrance on Rue Ste-Catherine).* ☎ *514/846-6577. www.montreal.anglican.org/ cathedral. Free self-guided tours in English and French.*

⑪ **Rue Ste-Catherine.** Though Montréal's nightlife may center on Boulevard St-Laurent and Rue Crescent, the heart of the city is Ste-Catherine, which pumps life and excitement into the surrounding areas day and night. The bars, theaters, strip clubs (the gigantic and gaudy sign marking Club Super-sexe unfortunately constitutes a large part of the street's unsaintly identity), countless buskers, and endless stretches of shops that line this famous thoroughfare make it absolutely fascinating for strolling and people-watching.

⑫ Place Ville-Marie. Legendary architect I.M. Pei designed this immense building (completed in 1962) and it's now one of the highlights of the city's skyline. The shape of the building is meant to recall Cartier's cross, planted on Mont-Royal to claim the island for France, and for de Maisonneuve's first little settlement, Ville-Marie. Before you browse the retail complex below, be sure to take a minute to examine the main floor's fountain, *Feminine Landscape* (1972), which was designed by Toronto artist Gerald Gladstone. *Intersection of Bd. Rene-Levesque and Rue University. www.placevillemarie.com.*

⑬ Fairmont The Queen Elizabeth. It may not be as historic as the Ritz or as glitzy as the Sofitel, but Montréal's largest hotel (1,039 rooms, in all) is one of downtown's best. And its location, right above Gare Central, can't be beat. The hotel opened in 1958 has had its share of historic moments. In 1969 John Lennon wrote and recorded "Give Peace a Chance" in suite 1742. And more than 50 heads of state bedded down in the hotel's lovely rooms when the Fairmont served as the headquarters for the 1976 Summer Olympic Games. *900 bd. Rene-Levesque. See p 126.*

⑭ ★★ Cathedrale Marie-Reine-du-Monde (Mary Queen of the World Cathedral). The second bishop of Montréal, Ignace Bourget (1799–1885), honored with a statue outside the cathedral's entrance, was the moving force behind this quarter-sized replica of St. Peter's Basilica in Rome. Many citizens decried the bishop's choice of location, in what was then the heart of a Protestant

Place Ville-Marie, designed by I.M. Pei is one of downtown's most important architectural landmarks.

quarter, but Bourget persisted and the cathedral was eventually completed in 1894. The dome is the cathedral's most impressive feature, but do note the statues on the roof, which commemorate the patron saints of local parishes. ⏱ *1 hr. 1085 rue de la Cathedrale.* ☎ *514/866-1661. www.cathedrale catholiquedemontreal.org. Free admission. Open Mon–Fri 7am–7:30pm; Sat 7:30am–8:30pm; Sun 8:30am–7:30pm.*

The beautiful Cathedrale Marie-Reine-du-Monde was built to resemble Rome's St. Peter's Basilica.

Mont-Royal

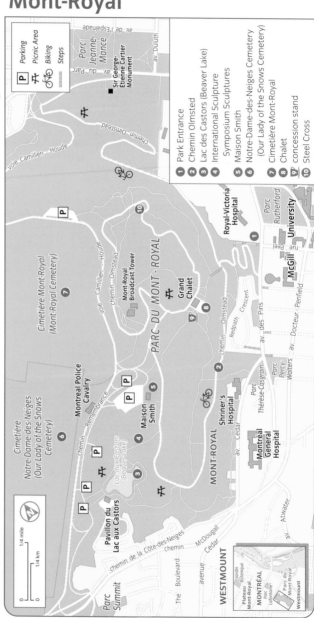

P Parking
Ⓟ Picnic Area
🚲 Biking
⸺ Steps

1 Park Entrance
2 Chemin Olmsted
3 Lac des Castors (Beaver Lake)
4 International Sculpture Symposium Sculptures
5 Maison Smith
6 Notre-Dame-des-Neiges Cemetery (Our Lady of the Snows Cemetery)
7 Cimetière Mont-Royal
8 Chalet
9 concession stand
10 Steel Cross

Montréal's largest green space may also be the most tax-ing on a sightseer's legs, possessing some rather steep hills and staircases. That said, you need only be in reasonably good shape to tackle this 200-hectare (494-acre) park, which was created in 1876 according to a plan by American landscape architect Frederick Law Olmsted (1802–1903), who also designed Central Park in New York City. The panoramas provided by the park should not be missed. START: **Rue Peel and Avenue des Pins.**

① Park Entrance. Consult the handy map at this site to get your bearings. To make this tour accessible to all, it follows a middle-of-the-road route through the park that should satisfy both the energetic and those who might not be up to challenging the park's steepest paths and hills. *Corner of Rue Peel and av. des Pins.*

② Chemin Olmsted. This broad, graveled path was named for the park's designer, and it's actually the only part of his design that became a reality (the rest of the park wasn't completed to his scheme).

Olmsted designed the road, the park's main artery, at such a gradual grade to accommodate pedestrians, and to help the horses pulling loads up and down the park's hills. Today, mountain bikers, joggers, mounted policemen, and hikers all cross paths here. An added plus: The road

Scenic Beaver Lake is a popular spot for outdoor enthusiasts year-round.

is closed to vehicular traffic, making it a joy for those wanting an uninterrupted stroll.

③ ★ Lac des Castors (Beaver Lake). During the summer, scores of sunbathers and picnickers usually cover the grassy swaths surrounding Beaver Lake, which itself is populated by paddle-boats and geese. However, when the mercury drops and snow falls, the geese are replaced by Montréalers on ice-skates—an artificial ice rink is set up adjacent to the lake every winter (the lake itself isn't strong enough to support skaters when frozen). The nearby pavilion rents out skates and even features a bronzed pair near the entrance that belonged to Jean Beliveau, a revered hockey player for the Montréal Canadiens. Beliveau wore this very pair of CCM Tackaberry skates when he notched his 500th goal in 1971.

④ International Sculpture Symposium Sculptures. On the grassy rise between Beaver Lake and Maison Smith sit several stone and metal structures that should grab your attention. These sculptures were erected in 1964 as part of the International Sculpture Symposium in Montréal. A collection of artists from various countries was given marble, granite, and/or metal with which to shape their abstract visions. One caveat was that they had a limited amount of time to complete their work. The marble representation of four priestesses, done by Geracimos Sklavos (1927–1967), is one of the

most striking pieces. Made of Italian marble, it was the second slab that the renowned Greek sculptor worked on—his initial material was deemed defective and had to be replaced. Not far from the sculptures, see if you can find two granite plaques (two of a total of five such plaques spread around the park) that have poetic phrases or humorous quips by Montréaler Gilbert Boyer chiseled into the rock. One plaque romanticizes the park and his partner, with one phrase, roughly translated into English, reading, "Sometimes I close my eyes…I imagine that I am there. You laugh. I miss this a lot." *Near Beaver Lake.*

One of the International Sculpture Symposium works in Parc Mont-Royal.

5 ★★ Maison Smith. Built in 1858, the park's information center also has bathrooms, a cafe, and a set of educational displays that describe both the history and flora/fauna of Mont Royal. Even though there's a ton of info to wade through, the descriptions on each display are extremely interesting and they give you tons of facts that will enrich the rest of your walk through the park. Be sure to visit the basement before you leave. You'll find an impossible-to-miss slab that takes up just about half of the entire floor. The chunk of gabbro (a dark, coarse rock), smoothed over by an enormous glacier millions of years ago, now serves as an impressive, yet educational, decorative bathroom piece. *30 min. 1260 chemin Remembrance. www.lemontroyal.qc.ca. Free admission. Open Mon–Fri 9am–5pm, Sat–Sun 10am–6pm.*

6 Notre-Dame-des-Neiges Cemetery (Our Lady of the Snows Cemetery). Many famous Montréalers have been laid to rest in the city's largest (and mostly Catholic) cemetery. Most notable are the Molson crypts, where members of the influential Canadian brewing family have been buried. Other prominent residents of the cemetery include statesman Sir George Etienne Cartier; poet Emile Nelligan; Calixa Lavallée, who composed Canada's national anthem; and famed hockey star, Maurice "The Rocket" Richard. Should you wish to find a specific grave, the cemetery's website offers a decent search function that will let you locate it. *4601 chemin Côte-des-Neiges. ☎ 514/735-1361. www.cimetierenddn.org.*

7 Cimetière Mont-Royal. Smaller than its neighbor, Mont Royal Cemetery was founded in 1852 by a group of Christian (but non-Catholic) denominations. The beautifully terraced cemetery was designed to resemble a garden and

The peaceful and beautifully landscaped Cimetière Mont-Royal is the final resting place of many of the city's Protestant residents.

Montreal's famous Steel Cross sits atop Mont-Royal.

makes for peaceful strolling. The most famous person to find eternal rest here? Anna Leonowens, the British governess who was the real-life inspiration behind *The King and I*. *1297 chemin de la Fôret*.

8 ★★ **Chalet.** The view from this lookout's terrace is one of the best in the city, and a few telescopes are available so you can make a more detailed study of the skyscrapers dotting the city's skyline and the St. Lawrence River. The chalet itself, built in 1932 at a then-astronomical cost of C$230,000, now hosts receptions, parties and concerts; the cafe inside sells drinks, ice cream, and snacks to famished hikers. If you do venture inside, note the 17 paintings hanging just below the ceiling. They relate the history of the region as well as the story of the French explorations of North America. *Voie Camillien-Houde. Free admission. Daily 9am–5pm.*

The **9** **concession stand** in the chalet sells drinks, sandwiches, ice cream and other light fare. Heed the signs that ask patrons to refrain from feeding the Chalet's adorable (and often begging) squirrels. *In Chalet, Voie Camillien-Houde. No phone. $.*

10 ★ **Steel Cross.** Legend has it that Montréal-founder de Maisonneuve erected a wooden cross here in 1642. Today this illuminated metal cross, erected in 1924 when the original had decayed beyond repair, is one of the most revered structures in the city. Visible from most of the city's downtown streets, the cross is lit in different colors for different occasions; when the Vatican was in the process of choosing a new pope, the steel structure glowed purple to honor the event. As you reach the foot of the cross, observe the plaque installed just at the top of the hill. Back in 1992, some 12,000 schoolchildren buried a time capsule filled with messages and drawings here in celebration of the city's 350th birthday. If all goes according to plan, the capsule will be unearthed in 2142, when Montréal blows out 500 candles on its birthday cake. *Just south of Voie Camillien-Houde.*

View from the lookout of the Chalet Mont-Royal.

Underground City

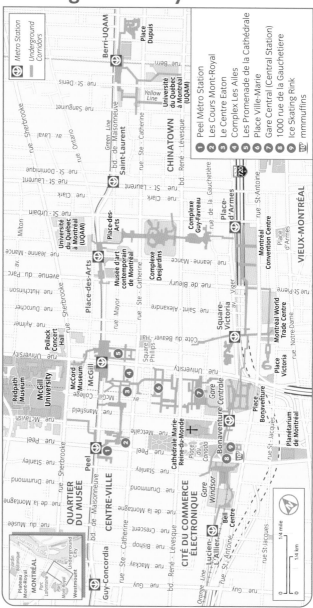

Legend
- 🔄 Metro Station
- Underground Corridors

1. Peel Métro Station
2. Les Cours Mont-Royal
3. Le Centre Eaton
4. Complex Les Ailes
5. Les Promenade de la Cathédrale
6. Place Ville-Marie
7. Gare Central (Central Station)
8. 1000 rue de la Gauchetiere
9. Ice Skating Rink
🔟 mmmuffins

Montréal's harsh, long winters (and hot and sticky summers) were the motivating force behind the construction of a series of underground tunnels that has created an accessible network of (mostly) subterranean shops, cafes, hotels, Métro stations, and attractions. This monumental achievement in urban planning stretches for nearly 32km (20 miles), and often sees nearly 500,000 people pass through its corridors each day. You can catch a movie, buy a new outfit, go ice-skating, take in some art, or hop on a train to New York City—all without ever venturing outdoors. START: **Peel Métro Station.**

① Peel Métro Station.
Note the colored circular artwork on the walls of this station by noted Québec artist Jean-Paul Mousseau (1927–1991). Mousseau, a member of the Automatist movement and a proponent of integrating art into urban landscapes, eventually became the art director for the Métro network, and contributed murals to several stations.

Colorful circular art on the walls of the Peel Métro station.

② ★ Les Cours Mont-Royal.
Cutting-edge fashion and trendy styles reign supreme in Les Cours Mont-Royal. "Three Monkeys" (p 71), perhaps the complex's best boutique, is a store that showcases some of Montréal's most talented independent artists and designers. A few of the other establishments pander to the young, clubbing crowd with loud and colorful outfits, but more demure yet chic shops give Les Cours Mont-Royal some fashion cred. Before it became a couture hot spot, the legendary Mont Royal Hotel stood on this spot from 1922 until the late '80s. It was then gutted and turned into today's complex of condos, offices, and boutiques. Now, instead of gawking at the beautiful hotel chandelier, visitors to Les Cours Mont-Royal can admire the "tingmiluks" in permanent flight above the atrium. First Nations artist David Piqtoukuni created the six metal sculptures of the flying shamans. *1455 rue Peel.*

③ Le Centre Eaton.
The hey-day of the once extraordinary Eaton Center has come and gone, but the four-level mall is the largest commercial space in downtown and is still one of the most popular places in the Underground City (it gets 19 million visitors a year). Its enormous food court might be one of the reasons. If you're looking for a fast-food fix, the endless sea of seats and eateries on the lowest level are a good option. *See p 54.*

First Nation sculptures hang from the ceilings at Le Cours Mont-Royal, a fashionable mall.

Ticket counters at Gare Central.

④ ★★ **Complex Les Ailes.** Connected to the Eaton Center is one of Montréal's most aesthetically impressive shopping centers. The former Eaton department store building (completed in 1927) was the second largest store in Canada before it was completely gutted in 1999 and turned into this office/retail complex. In addition to its anchor department store, Les Ailes de la Mode (p ###), the tri-level mall is also home to some of the city's priciest boutiques: Lacoste, Guess?, and Swarovski, to name a few. Its gorgeous skylight and illuminated atrium make the Complex Les Ailes a sight to see during the day as well as the evening. *677 rue Ste-Catherine ouest.* ☎ *514/288-3759. www.complexelesailes.com.*

⑤ **Les Promenade de la Cathédrale.** The layout of this 70-store mall may not be the most straightforward, but considering how it was constructed (the cathedral above it was "floated" on supports as the arcades below were built), it's understandable why the narrow paths twist and turn like they do. To visualize the unique and difficult birth of this retail complex, check out the series of visual displays depicting the construction process in its halls. *625 rue Ste-Catherine.* ☎ *514/849-9925.*

⑥ **Place Ville-Marie.** The city's first subterranean shopping mall debuted when this crucifix-shaped office building opened in 1962. Originally built to cover a rather unsightly railway trench north of Gare Central (bullet ⑦), the now-famous 41-story building—and the tunnels connecting it to both the train station and the Queen Elizabeth hotel (p 126)—eventually became the cornerstone of the network that evolved into the Underground City. See *p 47, bullet ⑫.*

⑦ **Gare Central (Central Station).** The current Central Station, which handles all of Montréal's major rail traffic, was built over the old Canadian Northern Railway's train tunnels. The tunnels date back to the 1920s, when several train stations were scattered throughout the city. When a consolidation of all the stations became necessary, construction on Gare Central began (though, thanks to delays caused by the Great Depression, the station wasn't completed until 1943). Adjacent to the station is **Les Halles de la Gare,** a

You can shop in the Underground City without having to worry about Montréal's fickle weather.

Skaters flock to the Ice rink at 1000 rue de la Gauchetiere.

shopping and restaurant complex that includes a branch of one of Montréal's best bakeries, La Premiere Moisson (p 97). *895 rue de la Gauchetiere ouest.* ☎ *514/989-2626.*

8 1000 rue de la Gauchetiere. There's some controversy as to whether this office tower is the tallest in the city (some skyscrapers have spires that exceed its height though the buildings are shorter). Even so, the 51-story post-modern structure (built in 1992) reaches Montréal's maximum allowance of 205m (672 ft.), the height of Mont Royal. Note the copper-capped roof and the rotunda entrances at the corner of the building's base—they were designed to mirror the design of the tower's northern neighbor, the Cathedral Marie-Reine-du-Monde (p 47, bullet **14**). *www.le1000.com.*

9 ★ Ice Skating Rink. Active folks might use this opportunity to show off their double toe loops or triple salchows, but it's more fun to grab a snack from one of the surrounding vendors and watch skaters dodge the columns in the middle of this indoor rink. The light-filled space—it lies just beneath a glass-domed atrium—was inspired by the rink in New York's Rockefeller Center. *See p 32, bullet* **3**.

After a couple of laps on the nearby ice rink, a strawberry-pecan muffin and a cup of Earl Grey from **10 mmmuffins,** a branch of a Canadian chain that sells tasty baked goods, always manages to put me back in a skating, and deliriously happy, mood. *1000 de la Gauchetiere (1st level).* ☎ *514/875-0791. Cash only. $.*

Extreme Weather in Montréal

Spring and fall barely exist in this city. For the most part, Montréal lives in either winter or summer—both seasons bringing with them very harsh weather. Winter lasts from November until late March, while June through September sees a sweltering summer. The cold months are synonymous with blizzards, frozen rain and, most devastating of all, ice storms. In 1998, one of the worst ice storms in history crippled the city by destroying power lines and leaving citizens to resort to their fireplaces for warmth. Summers, while not as destructive as winters, can be just as disagreeable. During the hottest months of July and August, the heat is coupled with stifling humidity. Luckily, the Underground City (mostly air-conditioned in the summer and blessedly heated in winter) helps keep Montréalers on an even keel.

Vieux-Montréal

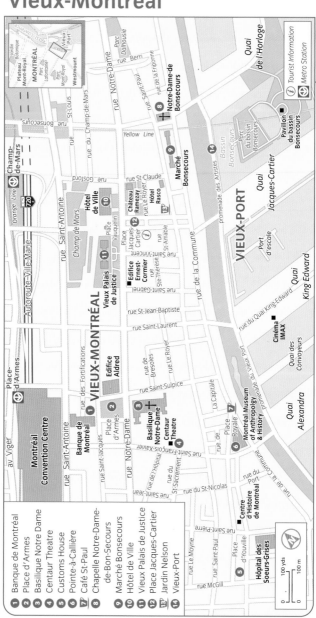

1 Banque de Montréal
2 Place d'Armes
3 Basilique Notre Dame
4 Centaur Theatre
5 Customs House
6 Pointe-à-Callière
7 Café St-Paul
8 Chapelle Notre-Dame-de-Bon-Secours
9 Marché Bonsecours
10 Hôtel de Ville
11 Vieux Palais de Justice
12 Place Jacques-Cartier
13 Jardin Nelson
14 Vieux-Port

Montréal's most visually distinct neighborhood also happens to be its most historic and intriguing. Strolling through this picturesque slice of old-world France, you can learn about the city's deep history and culture through its extraordinary museums and gorgeous architecture—all while soaking up the area's overwhelming charm. START: **Place d'Armes Métro Station.**

1 Banque de Montréal. This lavish neoclassical building was built in 1847. Though the exterior has remained largely unchanged, from 1901 to 1905 American architect Stanford White redid the interior, and in this enlarged space he created a vast lobby with high, green-marble columns topped with golden capitals. The public is welcome to stop in for a look, and is invited to explore the small banking museum that illustrates the bank's early operations (and houses one of only two $3 bills known to exist). ⏱ *30 min. 129 rue St-Jacques.* ☎ *514/877-6810. Free admission. Museum open Mon–Fri 10am–4pm.*

2 Place D'Armes. This pleasant cobblestone square's most prominent feature is the Maisonneuve Monument, commemorating a bloody 1644 confrontation in which French settlers—led by Montréal founder Paul Chomedey, sieur de Maisonneuve—defeated the native Iroquois tribe. In addition to a statue of Chomedey, the monument also features sculptures of three Montréal citizens from the same time period (note the dog next to one of them— his bark alerted the settlers to the impending invasion) and an Iroquois brave. *Intersection of Rue St-Jacques and Côte de la Place D'Armes.*

3 ★★★ Basilique Notre Dame. American architect James O'Donnell (the only person allowed burial in the basilica) bucked a trend towards neoclassicism when he designed this Gothic Revival masterpiece. The exterior is somewhat reminiscent of the cathedral in Paris with which it shares its name, but this basilica's stunning interior is what sets it apart from the famous French landmark. The magnificent altar (carved from rare linden wood), the vaulted ceiling (studded with 24-karat gold stars), the 12-ton bell (among the largest in North America), and the Limoges stained-glass windows (depicting moments from the city's history) are just some of the highlights that will fight for your attention when you step inside. *See p 12, bullet* **5**.

4 ★ Centaur Theater. Playbills replaced tickertape when this building was converted in 1965 from the city's stock exchange into the city's primary English-language theater. American architect George Post, who was also responsible for the New York Stock Exchange, designed

The Maisonneuve Monument and Basilique Notre Dame in Place D'Armes.

58

The Best Neighborhood Walks

the original Beaux Arts building in 1903. *See p 115.*

⑤ Customs House. Film buffs may remember this gargantuan building as the one that Robert DeNiro and Ed Norton broke into during the film *The Score*. Built of granite (the bottom three levels) and sandstone from 1912 to 1936, the Customs House is an imposing and austere structure. Although many Montréalers refer to this building as the Old Customs House or *Vieille Douane*, the first Customs House in the city was built on a site where a great deal of trading took place between the native Amerindians and Europeans and is now a part of Pointe-à-Callière (bullet ⑥). *400 place d'Youville.*

⑥ ★★★ Pointe-à-Callière. A few hundred years ago, this spot was completely submerged under the St. Pierre River. In 1645, the founders of the colony Ville-Marie built a fort here. Since then, the building has served as the home of Montréal governor Hector de Callière's (1648–1703), and now functions as the Montréal Museum of Archaeology and

The austere Customs House.

History. The museum also incorporates the pumping station across the street (now used as an interpretation center and exhibit of early 20th-century pumping equipment), and the complex is home to engaging exhibits and multimedia displays that trace the city's growth from a fledgling settlement to a burgeoning commercial city on the east coast.. ⏱ 1½ hr. *350 place Royal (corner of Rue de la Commune).* ☎ *514/872-9150. www.pacmuseum.qc.ca. Open Tues–Fri 10am–5pm, Sat–Sun 11am–5pm. June 24–Labour Day open until 6pm. Admission: C$12 adults, C$4.50 children 6–12, C$6.50 students, C$8 seniors (65+), C$25 families (1 adult, 3 children under 18 or 2 adults, 2 children under 18). Métro: Place d'Armes.*

The Pointe-à-Callière history museum sits on the exact location of the city's founding.

Stop by the very cozy ⑦ Café St-Paul for a latte, coffee, or one of their tasty milk shakes. The yummy sandwiches and salads will satisfy hungrier visitors. *143 rue St-Paul.* ☎ *514/844-7225. AE, MC, V. $–$$.*

⑧ ★★ Chapelle Notre-Dame-de-Bon-Secours. It's only fitting that a city so reliant on its location near a river has a church nicknamed the Sailors Church. Many survivors from some of the sea's worst tragedies have made a pilgrimage to this little chapel to give thanks for their good fortune (check out the ship models left hanging from the chapel's ceiling). Saint Margarite Bourgeoys, a pioneering nun,

A frieze from the exterior of the Vieux Palais de Justice.

founded the church in 1675 (though the present building dates to 1773). A museum about her life, as well as an archaeological site filled with artifacts, are located in a crypt below the chapel. ⏱ *1 hr. 400 rue St-Paul.* ☎ *514/282-8670. www.marguerite-bourgeoys.com. Open Tues–Sun: Mar–Apr 11am–3:30pm, May–Oct 10am–5:30pm, Nov–mid-Jan 11am–3:30pm. Closed mid-Jan–Feb. Free admission to chapel. Museum admission: C$6 adults, C$4 seniors and students, C$12 families (2 adults maximum); C$8 for access to museum/archaeological site.*

⑨ ★ Marché Bonsecours. Like so many of the landmark buildings in Old Montréal, Marché Bonsecours has been used for a variety of

A stature of the Virgin Mary presides over the Chapelle Notre-Dame-de-Bon-Secours, also known as the Sailors Church.

purposes. Completed in 1847, it has played home to the Parliament of United Canada, served as Montréal's City Hall, and morphed into a performance space for musicians. Though it's used today as an exhibition space, it mostly functions as a retail complex, housing a number of cafes and shops. It's most renowned, however, for its massive dome and the attention-grabbing architecture of its portico. *350 rue St-Paul.* ☎ *514/872-7730. www. marchebonsecours.qc.ca. Open Jan–Mar daily 10am–6pm; Apr–late June Sun–Wed 10am–6pm, Thurs–Fri 10am–9pm, Sat 10am–6pm; late June–Labour Day daily 10am–9pm; Labour Day–Oct, Sun–Wed 10am–6pm, Thurs–Sat 10am–9pm; Nov–Dec Sun–Wed 10am–6pm, Thurs–Fri 10am–9pm, Sat 10am–6pm.*

⑩ ★★ Hôtel de Ville. Architects Henri-Maurice Perrault and Alexander Cowper designed this ornate building in the mid-1800s. It's been Montréal's official City Hall since 1878, and it was here, in 1967, that French President Charles DeGaulle delighted Quebec separatists by shouting, *"Vive le Québec Libre!"* from the balcony (the Canadian government wasn't as amused). Don't just stand outside and gawk, as the interiors are impressive as well. The sculptures at the entry are *Woman with a Pail* and *The Sower,* both by Alfred Laliberté. ⏱ *1 hr. See p 13, bullet* ⑧.

⑪ Vieux Palais de Justice. Court sessions ceased here for good in 1978, when the newer Palais de Justice was erected next door, but the Old Court House still has municipal value, serving the city

Colorful Place Jacques-Cartier, named for the French explorer who discovered Canada, is home to many street vendors.

as a civic office building. Though the building was completed in 1856, the dome and the top floor were added much later in 1891 (take a close look and you'll be able to spot the differences). *155 rue Notre-Dame est.*

⑫ ★ **Place Jacques-Cartier.** Opened in 1804 as a marketplace, the bustling plaza known as Place Jacques Cartier is one of the area's most appealing. Entertaining performers fill the air with music and laughter, outdoor cafes serve as perches for people-watchers, and artists try to convince tourists to serve as their subjects. As you stroll past the 17th-century houses that line the promenade, observe the steeply pitched roofs, which were designed to shed heavy winter snows, and the small windows with double casements that let in light while keeping out wintry breezes. *South of Hotel de Ville, between Rue Notre Dame and Rue de la Commune.*

The best cafe from which to watch both the action at Place Jacques-Cartier and the water is at ⑬ **Jardin Nelson.** The menu lists a variety of pizzas, but you're best off indulging in one of their yummy crepes (C$14) as you enjoy the view. *407 place Jacques-Cartier.* ☎ *514/ 861-5731. www.jardinnelson.com. MC, V. $$.*

⑭ ★★★ **Vieux-Port.** Many who come to Old City naturally gravitate toward the port and to the walkways to the west. This time, when you reach the docks, locate the clock tower known as La Tour de l'Horloge (erected in 1922). From there you can admire the sights from one of its three (free) observation decks for a unique perspective of the St. Lawrence River. Once you descend from the tower, you can stroll through the Parc du Bassin Bonsecours or (for more adventurous travelers) you can try the jet boats that depart from the tower and whip through the furious Lachine Rapids. Rides last an hour, though your heart won't stop racing until long after you've stepped off the boat. Make sure you bring a change of clothes! A slightly tamer—and cheaper—speed boat offers a less drenching ride. ⏱ *2 hr. Saute Moutons–Clock Tower Pier (jet), Jacques Cartier Pier (speed).* ☎ *514/284-9607. www.jetboating montreal.com. Admission: Jet boat C$60 adults, C$50 youth (13-18), C$40 kids (6–12). Speed boat C$25 adults, C$20 youth (13–18), C$18 kids (6–12). Open May–Oct 10am–6pm, jet boats leave every 2 hr., speed boats leave every 30 min.* ●

Climb to the top of La Tour de l'Horloge in Vieux-Port and you'll be treated to a spectacular view of the city.

Shopping **Best Bets**

Best **Antiques**
★★ Monastiraki, *5478 bd. St-Laurent (p 66)*

Best **Store for Tracking Down That Rare Record**
★ Beatnick's, *3770 rue St-Denis (p 73)*

Best **Toy Store**
★★★ Atelier Toutou, *503 place d'Armes (p 74)*

Best **Gift Store**
★★ Mortimer Snodgrass, *209 rue St-Paul ouest (p 72)*

Best **Place for Men's and Women's High Fashion**
★★★ Holt Renfrew, *1300 rue Sherbrooke ouest (p 70)*

Best **Area of Town for High Fashion**
Rue Crescent

Best **Bookstore (New)**
★ Chapters, *1171 rue Ste-Catherine (p 67)*

Best **Bookstore (Used)**
★ The Word, *469 rue Milton (p 67)*

Best **Kitsch**
★★ Monastiraki, *5478 bd. St-Laurent (p 66)*

Best **Wine Shop**
SAQ Signature, *677 rue Ste-Catherine ouest (p 72)*

Best **Museum Shop**
★★ Musée d'Art Contemporain Boutique, *185 rue Ste-Catherine ouest (p 73)*

Best **Vintage Shopping**
Value Village, *2033 bd. Pie IX (p 71)*

Steve's Music is the best place in town to buy guitars and other musical instruments.

Best **Designer Vintage**
★★ Eva B, *2013 bd. St-Laurent (p 69)*

Best **Refurbished "Vintage"**
★★★ Preloved, *4832 bd. St-Laurent (p 71)*

Best **Budget Fashion**
Le Château, *1310 rue Ste-Catherine ouest (p 70)*

Best **Place for Musical Instruments**
★★ Steve's Music, *51 rue St-Antoine ouest (p 74)*

Best **Gourmet Food**
★ La Vieille Europe, *3855 bd. St-Laurent (p 72)*

Best **Food Market**
★★ Marché Atwater, *138 rue Atwater (p 72)*

Previous page: Cuisine Gourmet is Montréal's top spot for housewares.

Shopping **in Montréal**

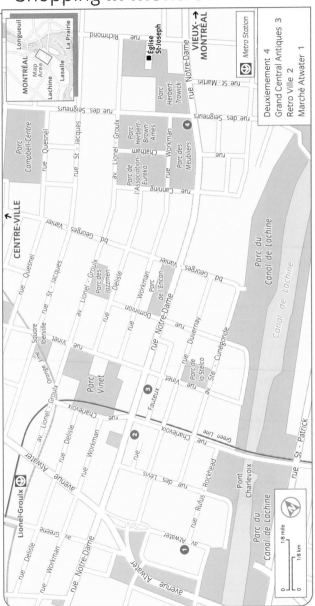

Deuxiemement 4
Grand Central Antiques 3
Retro Ville 2
Marché Atwater 1

Shopping **in Central Montréal**

MONTRÉAL
Longueuil
Lachine
Lasalle
La Prairie

ch. de la Côte-Ste-Catherine

Rosemont

Parc Père-Marquette

MILE END

1

av. Laurier

bd. St - Joseph

rue St - Denis

Laurier

Parc Sir-Wilfrid-Laurier

Papineau

2

PLATEAU MONT-ROYAL

av. du

Mont - Royal

Mont-Royal

Parc du Mont-Royal

Parc Jeanne-Mance

av. du Parc

Steel Cross

Monument Sir-George-Étienne Cartier

bd. St - Laurent

rue Rachel

3

4 5

av. Duluth

6
7

Parc Lafontaine

8

av. des Pins

9

10 11

12

13

Sherbrooke

14

Sherbrooke

15

rue St - Denis

Sherbrooke

LATIN QUARTER

Ontario

rue Amherst

Papineau

av.

McGill University

rue University

16

17

Place-des-Arts

rue St

LE VILLAGE

Papineau

Peel

McGill

St-Laurent

Berri-UQAM

bd. de Maisonneuve

Beaudry

CENTRE-VILLE

rue Ste - Catherine

18

19

CHINATOWN

bd. René - Lévesque

See Centre-Ville inset (right)

Bonaventure

Square-Victoria

Champ-de-Mars

720

20

Place-d'Armes

rue St - Antoine

21

rue Notre - Dame

VIEUX-MONTRÉAL

22

25

10

24

23

VIEUX-PORT

Île Sainte-Hélène

Parc Jean-Drapeau

Biosphere

Jean-Drapeau

Pont de la Concorde

Île Notre-Dame

0   1/4 mile
0   1/4 km

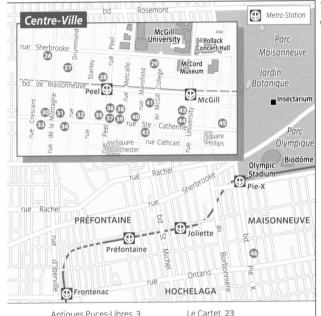

Montréal Shopping A to Z

Antiques & Collectibles
Antiques Puces-Libres
PLATEAU   The hike up St. Denis will be well worth the effort when you find that gorgeous 19th-century armoire in this fantastic shop. You'll also find the usual antique store offerings here like functional clocks, attractive vases, and other furniture. *4240 rue St-Denis.* ☎ *514/842-5931. AE, MC, V. Métro: Mont-Royal.*

★★ Deuxiemement VIEUX-MON-
TREAL   You'll find more than antiques at this regular on "Antique Alley," where a visit is warranted even if you're not interested in buying. You'll find nearly every imaginable object buried beneath the piles and piles of random secondhand stuff. *1880 rue Notre-Dame ouest.* ☎ *514/933-8560. No credit cards. Métro: Place d'Armes.*

Grand Central Antiques VIEUX-
MONTREAL   One of the most established vendors on "Antique Alley," Grand Central Antiques sells gorgeous, versatile pieces that could easily fit into the decor scheme of a Scottish castle or a

New York City loft. Restored furniture and decorations here are shiny and stately—with price tags to match. *2448 rue Notre-Dame ouest.* ☎ *514/935-1467. AE, MC, V. Métro: Champ-de-Mars.*

★ Les Artisans de Mueble
VIEUX-MONTREAL   This antique/art store in Old Montréal never seems to have more than a few customers at a time, making every visitor feel like he or she is the first to discover the expertly crafted products made by this small collective. As you wander the homey confines of the shop, take time to examine the handmade jewelry, woven quilts, antique furniture, and random bits of art. *88 rue St-Paul est.* ☎ *514/866-1836. AE, MC, V. Métro: Square Victoria.*

★★ Monastiraki MILE END   Play
the role of Alice as you enter a rabbit hole that's half antique store/half art gallery. Check out the bizarre art (most by Canadian artists) on the walls and the peculiar bric-a-brac strewn about the floor of this avant-garde wonderland. *5478 bd. St-Laurent.* ☎ *514/278-4879. No credit cards. Métro: Mont Royal.*

RETRO VILLE VIEUX-MONTREAL
Find the perfect retro embellishment for your pad in this unique Antique Alley store. Collectibles, memorabilia, vintage signs and old toys from the '50s, '60s and '70s are just some of the things you'll find in this cache of old treasures. *2652 rue Notre Dame ouest.* ☎ *514/939-2007. AE, DISC, MC, V. Métro: Champ-de-Mars.*

Art
Nicolin Gublin VIEUX-MONTREAL
Co-owned by artist Charlotte Nicolin (who favors marine life as the inspiration for her kooky and bold-colored paintings), this store might be

Nicolin Gublin sells quirky, aquatic-themed pieces.

La Baie, Canada's oldest retailer, has been in business for more than 115 years.

the closest thing Montréal has to a true aquarium. The shop also sells prints, posters, mugs, mouse pads and numerous other items imprinted with Nicolin's aquatically flavored work. *333 place d'Youville.* ☎ *514/844-3696. www.nicolin gublin.com. AE, MC, V. Métro: Square Victoria.*

Books
★ **Chapters** CENTRE-VILLE
Browse the extensive magazine racks on the bottom floor of this Canadian chain's tri-level flagship store, or grab a latte at the third-floor Starbucks (one of the few in downtown Montréal) as you flip through English and French paperbacks. *1171 rue Ste-Catherine ouest.* ☎ *514/849-8825. AE, MC, V. Métro: Peel.*

Paragraphe CENTRE-VILLE
Though it caters to university students seeking course materials, this storefront's many shelves are stocked with a decent selection of novels and classics. Once in a while the shop's couches are cleared out for in-store author appearances and small-scale musical performances. *2220 av. McGill College.* ☎ *514/845-5811. AE, MC, V. Métro: McGill.*

★ **The Word** CENTRE-VILLE   On pleasant days, you can peruse this cozy store's secondhand books, but you'll find business usually picks up in the colder months, when McGill University is in session. Though it's packed with college texts, it has its fair share of classics, too. *469 rue Milton.* ☎ *514/845-5640. No credit cards. Métro: McGill.*

Department Stores
La Baie (The Bay) CENTRE-VILLE
A branch of the Hudson Bay Company, Canada's oldest retailers (operating since 1692), this French-named

Maison Simons is known for its stylish clothes for both men and women. See p. 68.

Les Artisans de Mueble is a great source of handmade furniture and knickknacks. See p 66.

flagship has been in operation since 1891 and sells the usual department store fare: men's and women's clothing, beauty products, and housewares (including The Bay's famous wool blankets). *585 Ste-Catherine ouest.* ☎ *514/281-4422. www. hbc.com. AE, MC, V. Métro: McGill.*

★ Les Ailes de la Mode

CENTRE-VILLE   This aptly named department store—its moniker means "The Wings of Fashion"—sells both men's and women's designer labels constructed along clean lines and simple yet chic designs. The landmark building (built in 1927 as the flagship for the departed Eaton's department store) in which it resides is as impressive as the clothes themselves. *In the Complex Les Ailes, 677 rue Ste-Catherine ouest.* ☎ *514/282-4537. www.lesailes.com/en/accueil.htm. AE, MC, V. Métro: McGill.*

★ Maison Simons CENTRE-VILLE

You'll find the usual selection of department store fare here, but Simons rises above run-of-the-mill competitors thanks to its plethora of youthful labels and brands. Lines such as Le 31 (for men),

Contemporaine (for women), Twik (for younger women) feature playful, yet classic designs. *977 rue Ste-Catherine ouest.* ☎ *514/282-1840. AE, MC, V. Métro: Peel.*

Fashion

Aritmetik PLATEAU   A favorite of mine until they started pandering to the clubbing crowd, this local chain still manages to stay in touch with what's new in alternative fashion for men and women. Mannequins sport the latest from G-Star, Diesel, Kitchen Orange, and Stussy. *3688A bd. St-Laurent.* ☎ *514/985-4130. MC, V. Métro: St-Laurent.*

Bedo CENTRE-VILLE   Activists once targeted this store for its use of fur and leather, causing it to switch to breezier, less controversial materials. Today it puts out a casual clothing line for both men and women that's sophisticated without being stuffy. *1256 rue Ste-Catherine ouest.* ☎ *514/866-4962. AE, MC, V. Métro: Peel.*

★★ Boutique eXtc PLATEAU

Local denim labels such as Second and Guido Mary—only available in

Weekenders head to EnrgXchange for the latest in club attire. See p 69.

Montréal—are sold alongside other alternative clothing from such well-known names as Penguin and Lucky 7. It's extremely popular with university students and young locals looking to stock up on jeans or classic sneakers. *19 rue Prince Arthur.* ☎ *514/282-1083. AE, MC, V. Métro: St-Laurent.*

★★ Club Monaco CENTRE-VILLE Arguably a trendier analogue to Banana Republic, this Canadian-gone-global chain has a more refined edge, using simpler, bolder colors to sell the threads (for both sexes) off their somewhat pricey racks. *Les Cours Mont Royal, 1455 rue Peel, Suite 226.* ☎ *514/499-0959. www.clubmonaco.com. AE, MC, V. Métro: Peel.*

Dex PLATEAU   A shiny boutique with one-stop shopping for forward-thinking fashionistas. Good buys include carefully chosen European and Canadian casual labels, as well as classic sneakers and perfumes that'll give your outfit an aromatic

For the best in vintage clothing and costume masks, head to Eva B.

kick. *3651 bd. St-Laurent.* ☎ *514/286-3883. AE, MC, V. Métro: St-Laurent or Sherbrooke.*

EnrgXchange CENTRE-VILLE Come here to assemble your weekend clubbing outfits. A few high-end labels, such as Helmut Lang, are sold next to the racks of tight-fitting t-shirts and designer jeans. *In Les Cours Mont-Royal, 1455 rue Peel.* ☎ *514/282-0912. AE, MC, V. Métro: Peel.*

★★ Eva B QUARTIER LATIN   You'll rarely find an unsightly top or a defective pair of jeans amid the

Taxing Matters

Some of the best shopping in North America can be found in Montréal, but buyers will also be hit with ludicrous taxes. A 7% federal tax (known as TPS) is applied to most goods bought in Canada. In addition, a provincial tax of 8% (shown as TVQ on the receipt) is slapped on top of the already taxed subtotal. The good news: If your purchases (on a single receipt) total more than C$50 before taxes, you're entitled to a refund of both the TPS and TVQ.

To take advantage of this refund, request the booklet called *Tax Refund for Visitors to Canada* at duty-free shops, hotels, and tourist offices. It contains the necessary forms. Complete and submit them, with the *original* receipts (don't forget to make copies for your own records), within a year of the purchase. If you leave Canada by plane, train, bus, ferry, or boat, you'll have to attach your original boarding pass or travel ticket to the application. There has been talk of late about reducing both the federal and provincial taxes, so contact the Canadian consulate or Québec tourism office for up-to-the-minute information about taxes and rebates.

Roots is renowned for its stylish sportswear.

meticulously picked vintage clothing on this store's racks. Great selection does come at a slight premium: Many of the items are costlier than regular thrift store merchandise, though you can score that perfect jacket without breaking the bank if you look carefully enough. *2013 bd. St-Laurent.* ☎ *514/849-8246. MC, V. Métro: St. Laurent.*

★★★ **Holt Renfrew** CENTRE-VILLE After starting life as a furrier in 1837, Holt Renfrew has evolved to become a stop for clothes shoppers with big budgets and big taste. Gucci, Giorgio Armani, and Prada are just a few of the designer labels you'll find here. *1300 rue Sherbrooke ouest.* ☎ *514/ 842-5111. AE, DC, MC, V. Métro: Peel.*

★★ **Ima** PLATEAU   Dresses and tops with inventive patterns and sleek lines will grab your attention, but the high prices might scare your account-ant. Still, those price tags allow Ima to keep its racks full of obscure, yet ultra-fashionable labels. *24 rue Prince Arthur.* ☎ *514/844-0303. AE, MC, V. Métro: St-Laurent.*

★ **Jacob** CENTRE-VILLE   A mix of youthful casual wear and sophisti-cated, yet modern outfits that would work for both a conference room and a sidewalk cafe. *1220 Ste-Catherine ouest.* ☎ *514/861-9346. AE, MC, V. Métro: Peel.*

Le Château CENTRE-VILLE Budget shoppers with this store's trademark blue, red, and yellow plastic shopping bags are a familiar sight on rue Ste-Catherine. The bags are usually filled with inexpensive (but not cheap-looking) basics and sportswear for both men and women. *1310 rue Ste-Catherine ouest.* ☎ *514/866-2481. AE, MC, V. Métro: Peel.*

★★ **Lola & Emily** PLATEAU   One of the most popular boutiques for women's clothing in the Plateau, this store takes classic patterns and gives them an alternative and femi-nine twist without going overboard. Graceful and sleek dresses, asymmet-rical skirts, and various types of fab-rics make for some very intriguing options. *3475 bd. St-Laurent.* ☎ *514/ 288-7598. www.lolaandemily.com. AE, MC, V. Métro: St-Laurent.*

★ **L'Uomo** CENTRE-VILLE   L'Uomo specializes in fine men's Italian suits, with silky jackets and pants from such names as Versace, Cerruti, Dolce & Gabbana, and Armani. Perfect for impressing the beautiful people who make up its clientele. *1452 rue Peel.* ☎ *514/844-1008. www.luomo-montreal.com. AE, DC, DISC, MC, V. Métro: Peel.*

★★ **Ogilvy** CENTRE-VILLE
Founded in 1866, Ogilvy is steeped
in tradition, from its famous Christmas window displays to the daily
bagpiper that marches through the
premises at lunch. The historic store
is now home to such fashion-forward
names as Michael Kors, Burberry,
Hugo Boss, and Lacoste. *1307 rue
Ste-Catherine ouest.* ☎ *514/842-
7711. www.ogilvycanada.com. AE,
MC, V. Métro: Peel.*

★★★ **Preloved** PLATEAU
Preloved culls jeans, tops, and
dresses from local secondhand
shops; cuts them up; mixes and
matches the different pieces; sews
them back together; and then sells
the funky (and expensive) result to
trendy locals and celebs (including
Kate Hudson). *4832 bd. St-Laurent.*
☎ *514/499-9898. www.preloved.ca.
AE, MC, V. Métro: Mont-Royal.*

Roots CENTRE-VILLE   Fancy some
of the clothes seen on the athletes
at the last Olympics? In addition to
outfitting a number of countries'
summer and winter Olympic teams,
this Canadian company has also
churned out stylish casual wear for
the masses since 1973. *1035 rue
Ste-Catherine ouest.* ☎ *514/845-
7995. www.roots.com. AE, MC, V.
Métro: Peel.*

★ **space fb** PLATEAU   Style at
space fb isn't compromised by the
simple fabric selection, ensuring that
its sporty but classic outfits never
look bland or trashy. The American
Apparel of the north sells mostly
tank tops, hoodies, and other essen-
tials. *3632 bd. St-Laurent.* ☎ *514/
282-1991. www.spacefb.com. AE,
MC, V. Métro: St. Laurent.*

Sports Experts CENTRE-VILLE
Replace your torn parka or missing
swim shorts at the city's largest general sporting goods store. This well-
known Canadian chain has a great
selection of sports equipment,

outerwear, and camping gear, and
also restrings racquets and sharpens
skates. *930 rue Ste-Catherine ouest.*
☎ *514/866-1914. www.sports
experts.ca. AE, MC, V. Métro: McGill.*

★★★ **Three Monkeys** CENTRE-
VILLE   Betty Blush, Hastings +
Main, and Travis Taddeo are just
some of the creative clothing lines
on display at Three Monkeys. Committed to showcasing the best of
Montréal's independent designers,
the store is rife with edgy t-shirts,
fiercely cut denim, and tops that
usually require a second look to take
in their unique design. *In Les Cours
Mont Royal, 1455 rue Peel, Suite
217.* ☎ *514/284-1333. www.three
monkeys.ca. MC, V. Métro: Peel.*

Value Village EAST MONTREAL
Reminiscent of a Salvation Army
thrift store, Value Village also sells
cheap household goods, but shoppers come to this Canadian chain
for its surprisingly good selection of
secondhand clothing. The only time
there are massive crowds is during
Halloween, when Value Village
becomes the target of wanna-be
vampires, clowns, and fairies. *2033
bd. Pie IX.* ☎ *514/528-8604. www.
valuevillage.com. Cash only. Métro:
Pie IX.*

★★ **Zara** CENTRE-VILLE   Urbane
and modern, this Spanish-owned
clothing company isn't afraid to use

*The selection of treats at Au Festin de
Babette will satisfy even the choosiest
of chocoholics. See p. 72.*

subtle yet forward-thinking embellishments and twists in their sharp looks for both men and women. Prices are a little high, but are significantly less than what you'd pay at comparable boutiques. *1500 av. McGill College.* ☎ *514/281-2001. AE, MC, V. Métro: McGill.*

Edibles
★ Au Festin de Babette
PLATEAU   Take a seat at one of this boutique's colorful pastel tables and ponder the culinary gift options (perhaps some Michel Cluziel chocolates?) over ice cream and tea. If you're still unsure, you can't go wrong with the sinfully creamy Earl Grey chocolates. *4085 rue St- Denis.* ☎ *514/849-0214. MC, V. Métro: Sherbrooke.*

Frenco Vrac PLATEAU   Poutine and smoked meat aren't exactly good for your heart, but your body will rejoice at this health food grocery. Whole grains, oats, wheat germ, and all sorts of fiber-rich foodstuffs are dispensed from plastic towers, and the organic and natural medicines behind the counter might help you with the heartburn from Schwartz's. *3985 bd. St-Laurent.* ☎ *514/285-1319. MC, V. Métro: St-Laurent.*

★ La Vieille Europe
PLATEAU Create the mother of all quickie-lunches with the wide selection of

Mortimer Snodgrass is a prime spot for informal gifts.

delectable cheeses, salty cold cuts, and savory coffees sold at this store. The gourmet fare is imported mostly from England, France, and Germany—your taste buds won't be disappointed. *3855 bd. St-Laurent.* ☎ *514/842-5773. MC, V. Métro: St-Laurent.*

★★ Le Cartet VIEUX-MONTREAL Before they head off to work, some locals gather in the small eating area at this fantastic *"boutique alimentaire"* for their coffee and paper. Others come for the tasty gourmet products stacked on the shelves, including sauces and condiments, coffee supplies, and various delicacies. *106 rue McGill.* ☎ *514/871-8887. MC, V. Métro: Square Victoria.*

★★ Marché Atwater CENTRE-VILLE   Strolling past the aromatic goods displayed by the butchers, bakers, pastry chefs, and grocers in Marché Atwater is à great way to work up an appetite. Arguably the best place to pick up all the fixings for that killer dinner you're planning to cook. *138 rue Atwater.* ☎ *514/ 937-7754. Most vendors don't take credit cards. Métro: Lionel Groulx.*

SAQ CENTRE-VILLE   Alcohol, not including beer, is heavily regulated by the provincial government and sold in four different SAQ outlet types: "Express" holds the most popular libations and is open until 10pm, "Classique" has more variety but closes earlier, "Selection" brags of having the most variety of wines, and "Signature" (whose only location is in the Complex Les Ailes de la Mode) has the rarest and most expensive libations in the city. *SAQ Signature: 677 rue Ste-Catherine ouest.* ☎ *514/ 282-9445. www.saq.com. AE, MC, V. Métro: McGill.*

Gifts
★★ Mortimer Snodgrass
VIEUX-MONTREAL   The unusual name usually prepares shoppers for

Beatnick's is a prime spot for picking up old music releases.

what's inside: loud vinyl handbags, quirky tools, children's clothing with humorous phrases emblazoned across the chest or bum, and funky neon alarm clocks. You might not find a gift for that ultra-conservative cousin of yours, but for everyone else Mortimer Snodgrass has something that will make them smile. *209 rue St-Paul ouest.* ☎ *514/499-2851. www.mortimersnodgrass.com/en. AE, MC, V. Métro: Place d'Armes or Square Victoria.*

★★ **Musée d'Art Contemporain** CENTRE-VILLE Museum gift shops are usually stocked with useless coffee table books or prints that will eventually collect a layer of dust in your attic. The boutique at the Musee d'Art Contemporain breaks that trend with tastefully designed vases, clocks, and other types of housewares—though you'll also find stationery and the museum-standard collection of prints and posters. *185 rue Ste-Catherine ouest.* ☎ *514/ 847-6904. www.macm.org. AE, MC, V. Métro: Place des Arts.*

Housewares
Cuisine Gourmet CENTRE-VILLE The flagship of a Montréal-based housewares chain, this is one of the largest stores in Canada for cookware and kitchen accessories. Among the 35,000 items in stock, you'll find Riedel wine glasses, All-Clad pans, Calphon cutlery, and other excellent utensils. *2005 rue Drummond.* ☎ *514/845-2112. www.cuisine gourmet.com. AE, MC, V. Métro: Peel.*

Jewelry
bleu comme le ciel CENTRE-VILLE This boutique's flashy costume jewelry is perfect for women looking to shake up their image. The bulk of the reasonably priced merchandise reveals a Middle Eastern/ North African influence. *2000 rue Peel. AE, MC, V.* ☎ *514/847-1128. Métro: Peel.*

Music
Archambault Musique QUARTIER LATIN I could easily spend an entire afternoon playing the guitars and bongos on this store's second floor, or browsing the huge selection of English and French CDs on the ground floor. There's also a good selection of Québecois albums that you won't find outside of the region. *500 rue Ste-Catherine est.* ☎ *514/849-6201. AE, MC, V. Métro: Berri-UQAM.*

★ **Beatnick's** PLATEAU The storefront at this Everyman's record store hasn't changed much in the last decade, but it's what's inside that brings back its faithful and loyal customers. Selection is more varied and you might even be able to score that highly sought-after '60s release you've always wanted. *3770 rue St–Denis.* ☎ *514/842-0664. www. beatnickmusic.com. MC, V. Métro: Sherbrooke.*

★ **Inbeat** PLATEAU   The mini-fridge full of Red Bull and the dark setup at this vinyl store are indicative of its status as the place where Montréal's hardcore DJs go to prospect for that elusive sample. Non-DJs will score some worthwhile discs here, but they'll mostly find sub-genres of electronica and drum 'n' bass. *3814 bd. St-Laurent.* ☎ *514/499-2063. www.inbeatmusic.com. MC, V. Métro: Sherbrooke.*

★★ **Steve's Music** VIEUX MON-TREAL   There are a few other instrument shops in town, but Steve's Music reigns supreme as the city's only stop for musicians when it comes to selection. Names such as Alvarez, Guild, Taylor, Martin, Fender, PRS, and Gibson all have guitars hanging somewhere in the store, and drums, keyboards, and other instruments are also sold here.

51 rue St-Antoine ouest. ☎ *514/878-2216. www.stevesmusic.com. MC, V. Métro: Place d'Armes.*

Toys

★★★ **kids** **Atelier Toutou (Plush Factory)** VIEUX-MONTREAL   Young kids get to choose a stuffed animal from a wide selection, and then pick out accessories and clothing for their new friend before the staff here sews everything together. The finished product is given to children complete with a "passport"—a document with the cuddly beast's name, date of birth, description, and even a picture with its new owner. *503 place d'Armes.* ☎ *514/288-2599. www. plushfactory.com. MC, V. Métro: Place d'Armes.*

★ **kids** **La Grande Ourse** PLATEAU   Authenticity is something taken for granted with children's toys, but La Grande Ourse sells handcrafted wooden toys, mostly for toddlers, that range from rocking horses to castles. You'll also find stuffed animals and dolls made from only natural fibers. *263 av. Duluth est.* ☎ *514/847-1207. Cash only. Métro: Sherbrooke.* ●

Children adore making their own stuffed animals at Atelier Toutou (Plush Factory).

Parc du Mont-Royal & McGill U.

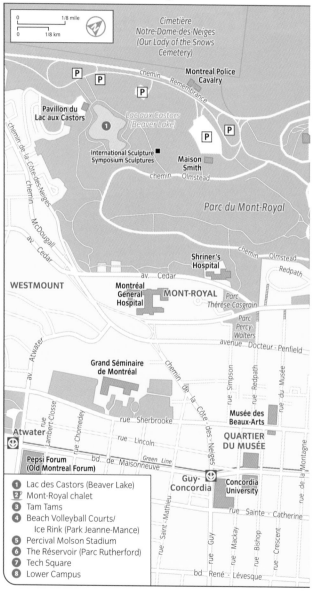

0   1/8 mile
0   1/8 km

Cimetière
Notre-Dame-des-Neiges
(Our Lady of the Snows
Cemetery)

Montreal Police
Cavalry

P

P

P

chemin

Remembrance

P

P

Pavillon du
Lac aux Castors

Lac aux Castors
(Beaver Lake)

❶

International Sculpture
Symposium Sculptures

Maison
Smith

chemin   Olmstead

chemin de la Côte-des-Neiges

chemin

McDougall

av.   Cedar

Parc du Mont-Royal

chemin   Olmstead

Redpath

Shriner's
Hospital

av.   Cedar

WESTMOUNT

Montréal
General
Hospital

MONT-ROYAL

Parc
Thérèse-Casgrain

Parc
Percy-
Walters

avenue   Docteur - Penfield

Grand Séminaire
de Montréal

chemin   de   la   Côte-des-Neiges

rue   Simpson

rue   Redpath

rue   du   Musée

av.   Atwater

rue   Lambert-Closse

rue   Chomedey

rue   Sherbrooke

Musée des
Beaux-Arts

rue   Lincoln

QUARTIER
DU MUSÉE

Atwater

Ⓜ

Pepsi Forum
(Old Montreal Forum)

bd.   de   Maisonneuve

Green   Line

Guy-
Concordia

Ⓜ

Concordia
University

rue   de   la   Montagne

❶ Lac des Castors (Beaver Lake)
❷ Mont-Royal chalet
❸ Tam Tams
❹ Beach Volleyball Courts/
   Ice Rink (Park Jeanne-Mance)
❺ Percival Molson Stadium
❻ The Réservoir (Parc Rutherford)
❼ Tech Square
❽ Lower Campus

rue   Saint - Mathieu

rue   Guy

rue   Mackay

rue   Bishop

rue   Crescent

rue   Sainte - Catherine

bd.   René - Lévesque

Previous page: Two people out for a stroll in Parc Lafontaine.

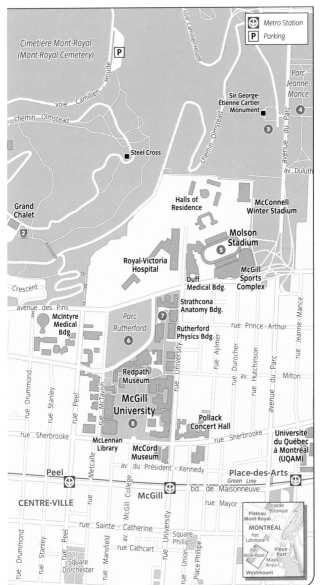

Metro Station
P Parking

Cimetière Mont-Royal
(Mont-Royal Cemetery)

P

voie Camillien

chemin Olmstead

voie Camillien-Houde

Parc
Jeanne-
Mance
4

Sir George-
Étienne Cartier
Monument
3

avenue du Parc

av. Duluth

Steel Cross

chemin Olmstead

Grand
Chalet
2

Halls of
Residence

McConnell
Winter Stadium

Molson
Stadium
5

Royal-Victoria
Hospital

Duff
Medical Bdg.

McGill
Sports
Complex

Crescent

avenue des Pins

McIntyre
Medical
Bdg.

Parc
Rutherford
6

7

Strathcona
Anatomy Bdg.

Rutherford
Physics Bdg.

rue Prince-Arthur

rue Aylmer

rue Durocher

av. Hutchinson

avenue du Parc

rue Jeanne-Mance

Milton

rue Drummond

rue Stanley

rue Peel

rue McTavish

rue University

Redpath
Museum

McGill
University
8

Pollack
Concert Hall

rue Sherbrooke

McLennan
Library

McCord
Museum

rue Sherbrooke

Université
du Québec
à Montréal
(UQAM)

Metcalfe

av. du Président-Kennedy

Peel

CENTRE-VILLE

rue McGill-College

McGill

Place-des-Arts

Green Line

bd. de Maisonneuve

rue Mayor

rue Drummond

rue Stanley

rue Peel

rue Mansfield

av. McGill-College

rue University

rue Sainte-Catherine

rue Cathcart

Square
Phillips

Place Phillip

rue Union

Square
Dorchester

Jardin
Botanique

Plateau
Mont-Royal

MONTRÉAL

Parc
Lafontaine

Parc
Mont-Royal

Map
Area

Westmount

Vieux-
Port

Montréal's two most visible green spaces loom large above the downtown area. Parc du Mont-Royal and the McGill University campus have become indelible parts of the urban sprawl cherished by both locals and visitors, not just for aesthetic reasons but for the recreational diversions they offer. START: **Peel Métro station, then walk to Avenue des Pins park entrance.**

1 ★ Lac des Castors (Beaver Lake). My preferred park sanctuary. Here, sunbathers laze on their towels, Mom and Dad chase their giggling children, and students leaf through trashy novels and magazines instead of their hefty textbooks. It's no wonder that you'll find very few free swaths of grass around the lake on pleasant summer days. Later in the year, when the grass is buried under a few feet of snow, locals trade in their sun block for skates and use the artificial ice rink that's put up annually next to the lake. *Northwest of Chemin Olmsted.*

The cafe inside **2 Mont-Royal chalet** will quench your thirst or sate any hunger pangs you felt on

One of the hundreds of drummers who flock to the park's Tam Tams jam session, held every Sunday in summer.

climbing up the massive set of stairs to get here. Drinks, ice cream, and tasty baked goods are all on the menu. Once you've refueled, make your way to the chalet's lookout for a spectacular view of downtown Montréal. *Chemin Olmsted. Open 9am–5pm. No phone. $.*

3 ★★★ Tam Tams. If you have a summer or spring Sunday to spare, don't miss this enormous gathering of hippies, locals, musicians, vendors, and fantasy combatants. Tam Tams is a collection of a few hundred drummers who congregate—generally, late in the morning—around the park's statue of Sir George-Étienne Cartier (p 20, bullet **4**). As a mass of random percussionists (the only qualification is that you have some instrument you can bang on) builds around the steps of the statue, the rest of the park fills with sunbathers and picnickers who turn the impromptu concert into a festive social event. You'll also find vendors hawking homemade jewelry and art as well as kooky LARPers (Live Action Role Players) putting on enormous fanciful faux battles with foam weapons in a grove of trees to the north. ⏲ *1½ hr. North of Av. du Parc and Rue Duluth.*

4 Beach Volleyball Courts/Ice Rink (Park Jeanne-Mance). If you'd rather break a sweat than lie in the sun, check out the park across the street from Mont-Royal. You'll find a baseball field, tennis courts, a football/soccer field and, best of all, beach volleyball courts. When the weather is acceptable, these giant sandboxes are full of shirtless players setting and spiking all the live-long day. The cold weather brings out an excellent ice-rink that's popular among shinny (just gloves, skates, and sticks) hockey players. I once played here when it was −40°C (−40°F) and there were still half a dozen players trooping it out. *Av. du Parc & Rue Duluth.*

5 Percival Molson Stadium. Home of the local pro football team, the popular Montréal Alouettes, this old concrete stadium may not be easy on the eyes (and the artificial turf isn't as attractive as natural grass, but fans aren't fazed one bit. During the season, the stadium consistently sells out, even on the coldest day in October, making it almost as rowdy and chaotic as the Bell Center during hockey playoffs. *Rue University and Av. des Pins.* ☎ *514/871-2255 for Alouettes tickets and info. www. alouettes.net. See p 120.*

6 The Réservoir (Parc Rutherford). Set between the McGill campus and Mont-Royal park is an enormous expanse of grass known to locals as The Réservoir (named for nearby McTavish water reservoir). Students come here to study on warm fall days, and it's one of the best spots for finding an ultimate Frisbee game. The university's club team practices and plays here, but you'll likely find pick-up games on other days. ⏲ *30 min. Rue McTavish and Av. des Pins.*

7 Tech Square. Just north of the spot where the Nobel Prize–winning "father of nuclear physics," Sir Ernest Rutherford (1871–1937), made some of his most profound discoveries is the area on McGill campus known as "Tech Square." Until recently, the cold and austere engineering and chemistry buildings here made for a sterile and at times depressing environment. But thanks to a generous gift from a McGill alumnus, the area got a much-needed face-lift. A tranquil yet modern fountain was created to fit in seamlessly with its surroundings and, along with the sharply designed Lorne Trottier building, has transformed Tech Square from an eyesore to an eye-catching location. *Rue University and Rue Prince-Arthur.*

8 ★ Lower Campus. Dotted with trees and small statues, the airy lower campus's huge green swaths are enjoyed by both locals and students. Frisbee and soccer players dominate the western quad while the more studious flip through physics textbooks under the shade of the trees in the east. Bookended by a gentle hill (the preferred perch for sunbathers) and football uprights, the western quad hasn't seen a McGill football game since the team moved to the Molson Stadium. Instead, it's the main site of convocation in the spring, and in winter it's a popular place for "broomball," a clumsy sport that's best described as "hockey without skates." ⏲ *1 hr. Rue Sherbrooke and Av. McGill College.*

Picturesque McGill University is one of the most prestigious institutions of learning in Canada.

The **Great** Outdoors

Parc Lafontaine

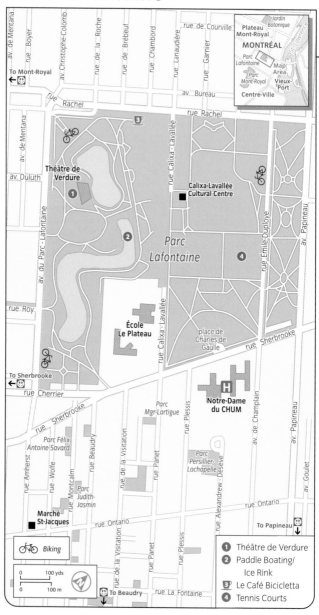

1	Théâtre de Verdure
2	Paddle Boating/ Ice Rink
3	Le Café Bicicletta
4	Tennis Courts

🚲 Biking

0	100 yds
0	100 m

Many locals come to this green oasis to take in a free show in the park's outdoor theater or to play in one of its two lakes. Most, however, simply want to escape the city by going to the one park in Montréal that actually feels removed from its chaotic streets. START: **Sherbrooke Métro station.**

1 ★★ Théâtre de Verdure. Sunset does not send visitors to Parc Lafontaine scurrying for the exits. Instead, most people stay here after dark because of this excellent, open-air theater—one of the best places to see a show in Montréal. Summer evenings always feature some form of free entertainment: French films, ballet performances, music concerts, and more. Instead of bringing your bottle of Shiraz to a restaurant on St-Denis, pack it in a picnic basket and have a wonderfully relaxing dinner as you watch a free show under the night sky. ⏱ *10 min. See p 115.*

2 ★ Paddle Boating/Ice Rink. Various waterfowl float around aimlessly in the two man-made ponds set in the middle of Parc Lafontaine. Humans like to take to the water here as well. During the summer, there's nothing more peaceful than renting a paddle boat and cycling lazily around the delightful ponds. When the water freezes over in winter, visitors bring their toques and ice skates for some frigid aerobic activity in the lit, music-filled ice rinks. Forgot your skates at home? Rent them pond-side at the skate rental kiosk. ⏱ *1 hr.*

A favorite of cyclists, the aptly named **3 Le Café Bicicletta** is also frequented by locals and visitors to Parc Lafontaine. This cozy cafe serves everything from yummy empanadas to robust espressos. In summer, head to the cafe's laid-back terrace, order some fantastic pastries, and while the afternoon away over a few cups of coffee. *1251 rue Rachel E. (Maison des Cyclistes).* ☎ *514/521-8356. $.*

4 Tennis Courts. The 14 courts in Parc Lafontaine are in decent condition and are the most convenient option in downtown Montréal for tennis enthusiasts. Open until 10pm, the lit courts can sometimes get crowded, but try to score an evening session if you can. Thanks to the oppressive summer humidity, playing in the cooler Montréal nights is far more comfortable than hitting aces in the light of day. Reservations aren't required, but you'll have to sign up for a slot at the courts or you can call ahead of time (☎ 514/872-3626) to make sure you get the slot you want. ⏱ *1 hr. East end of Parc Lafontaine.*

Free summer evening performances attract throngs to the Théâtre de Verdure.

Parc Jean Drapeau

1 Lachine Canal Bike Path
2 Casino de Montréal
3 Floralies Gardens
4 Circuit Gilles Villeneuve
   (Canadian Grand Prix)
5 Biosphere
6 Musée David M. Stewart
7 La Ronde

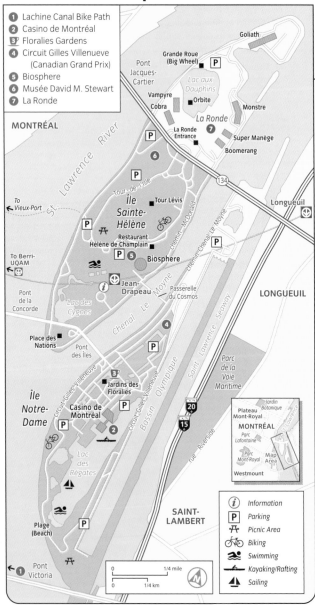

MONTRÉAL

Lawrence River
St.

To Vieux-Port

To Berri-UQAM

Pont Jacques-Cartier

Goliath

Grande Roue (Big Wheel)

Lac aux Dauphins

Vampyre
Cobra
Orbite
La Ronde
Monstre
La Ronde Entrance
Super Manège
Boomerang

Île Sainte-Hélène
Tour-de-l'Isle
Tour Lévis
Restaurant Hélène de Champlain
Biosphere
Jean-Drapeau
Passerelle du Cosmos

chemin McDonald
chemin Chenal-Le Moyne

Longueuil

LONGUEUIL

Pont de la Concorde

Lac des Cygnes

Chenal Le Moyne

Place des Nations
Pont des Iles

Île Notre-Dame
Circuit Gilles Villeneuve

Jardins des Floralies

Casino de Montréal

Lac des Régates

Bassin Olympique

Saint Lawrence Seaway

Parc de la Voie Maritime

rue Riverside

Jardin Botanique
Plateau Mont-Royal
MONTRÉAL
Parc Lafontaine
Parc Mont-Royal
Map Area
Westmount

Plage (Beach)

SAINT-LAMBERT

Pont Victoria

| 0 | | 1/4 mile |
| 0 | | 1/4 km |

(i) Information
P Parking
Picnic Area
Biking
Swimming
Kayaking/Rafting
Sailing

Taking up most of the man-made islands of Île Notre-Dame and Île Ste-Hélène on the St. Lawrence River, Parc Jean Drapeau is another favorite destination of Montréalers. In addition to the usual park offerings, a few thrill-seeking "extracurricular" activities include car-racing, gambling, and a first-rate theme park.

START: **Parc du Canal-de-Lachine (from Bonaventure Métro station, follow Rue Peel south).**

1 ★★ Lachine Canal Bike Path. It's true that the Lachine Canal bike path, which stretches for almost 15km (9 miles) along the St. Lawrence River, never really overlaps with Parc Jean Drapeau. But it's worth mentioning because it's one of Montréal's best outdoor spots and because Parc Jean Drapeau, while not associated with the path in any way, is accessible by this fantastic stretch of pavement. Skaters, bikers, and joggers should follow the bike path to Cite du Havre and look for the signs leading to Île Notre-Dame. It's a much more relaxing and picturesque way to get to the park than taking the Métro. ⏱ *30 min. South of Parc du Canal-de-Lachineue, Av. Pierre-Dupuy on Jetée Mackay. Métro: Bonaventure.*

2 Casino de Montréal. You may not get a workout here, but your wallet surely will. Over 3,200 slot machines, as well as blackjack, roulette, baccarat, craps, and various poker tables are available to siphon money out of your bank account. As far as North American casinos go, what's inside isn't that spectacular. The exterior is a different story. Built for Expo '67, two of the main buildings are lit at night to showcase its clamshell shape and the surrounding Venetian blind–like embellishments. ⏱ *1 hr. 1 av. du Casino. www.casino-de-montreal.com.* ☎ *514/392-2746. Open 24 hr. Métro: Île Ste-Hélène. Shuttle available from Métro station. See p 119.*

Though there is a snack bar where you can get drinks and light fare in **3 Floralies Gardens,** you're better off packing a picnic lunch to eat as you kick back and relax on this gorgeous 4.8-hectare (12-acre) oasis. The gardens were created in 1980 as part of a competition between respected international artists and landscapers. *Île Notre-Dame.*

4 Circuit Gilles Villenueve (Canadian Grand Prix). Since 1978, when the Grand Prix moved permanently to Montréal, checkered flags have waved outside every store-front in the downtown area to celebrate the arrival of the racers and their teams. The circuit itself snakes

Cycling the Lachine Canal Bike Path is one of Montréal's best outdoor experiences.

The Biosphere is home to a number of multimedia exhibitions on ecological issues.

through the northeastern part of Île Notre-Dame. Finding tickets to the late June race can be difficult (reserve months in advance), if not impossible. Try to score Bronze 22 tickets—the seats overlook superfast turn 13, where race cars usually scream by at speeds exceeding 241kmph (150mph). If you you'd rather see sharp turns and deft movements, opt for Bronze 31 tickets, which is the best spot for watching messy crashes and aggressive driving. When the open-wheel race cars leave the city, the track is converted to a public bike/skate path. ⏱ *10 min. Ile Notre-Dame.* www.grandprix.ca. ☎ *514/ 350-0000. Tickets C$50–C$200; 3-day (weekend) passes available. Métro: Île Ste-Hélène.*

5 Biosphere. This translucent globe usually intrigues travelers driving into Montréal in the evening or early morning thanks to its ghostly presence along the St. Lawrence River. If you're into extravagant visual shows or if you want to see a remarkable view of the river, it makes for a good stop. The attraction's multimedia displays and exhibitions pull the heartstrings of nature lovers as they examine the current state of the St. Lawrence ecosystem. ⏱ *45 min. 160 chemin Tour-de-l'Isle, Île Ste-Hélène.* www.biosphere.ec.gc.ca.

☎ *514/283-5000. Open noon–5pm Mon–Fri mid-Sept to mid-June, 10am– 6pm daily mid-June to mid-Sept. Admission: C$9.50 adult, C$7.50 students and seniors, C$5 youths 7–17, free for kids under 7, C$20 for families. Biosphere–Stewart Museum combination ticket available. Métro: Parc Jean-Drapeau.*

6 ★★ Musée David M. Stewart. Set on the old site of a 19th-century fort is this museum, which examines the history and development of Canada. Here you'll find various artifacts from the 16th- through 19th-centuries. The two exhibitions of note are the interactive physics exhibition showcasing the instruments of the French monk and physicist Abbé Nollet (1700–1770), and the Gunsmith's Gallery, which showcases over a thousand different firearms from the early 16th century to the present. The museum is also worth seeing for its re-enactments of battles and colonial life (though young kids might find them a bit frightening). ⏱ *1hr. Vieux Fort, Île Ste-Hélène.* www.stewart-museum.org. ☎ *514/861-6701. Admission: C$10 adults, C$7 students and seniors, free for kids under 7, C$20 for families (2 adults, 2 kids; or 1 adult, 3 kids). Biosphere-Stewart Museum combination ticket available. Open 10am–5pm daily mid-May to mid-Oct, 10am–5pm Wed–Mon mid-Oct to mid-May. Métro: Parc Jean-Drapeau.*

7 kids La Ronde. The city's only true amusement park. Thrill-seekers should try the hair-raising Goliath, the fastest (reaching almost 113kmph/70mph) and biggest roller coaster in Canada. Looking for something a little intense? Try the 20-year-old wooden roller coaster, Le Monstre. If you're here on weekends in July, be sure to attend the park's spectacular International Fireworks Competition. ⏱ *2 hr. See p 36, bullet* **1**. ●

Dining Best Bets

★★★ Best **Smoked Meat**
Schwartz's, $ 3895 bd. St-Laurent
(p 98)

Best **Bakery**
★ Premiere Moisson, $ 1490 rue
Sherbrooke ouest (p 97)

Best **Bagels**
★★★ St-Viateur, $ 1127 av. Mont
Royal (p 98)

Best **Sandwiches**
★ Santropol, $ 3990 St-Urbain
(p 97)

Best **Steaks**
★★ Moishe's, $$$$ 3961 bd.
St-Laurent (p 96)

Best **Caribbean**
L'Corridor, $ 3655 bd. St-Laurent
(p 94)

Best **Wood-Fired Pizza**
Pizzedelic, $$ 3509 bd. St-Laurent
(p 96)

Best **99-Cent Pizza**
1 and 1 Pizza, $ 3679 bd. St-Laurent
(p 90)

Best **Ice Cream**
Le Bilboquet, $ 1311 rue Bernard
ouest (p 94)

Best **"Hands-On" Experience**
Blue Nile, $$$ 3706 rue St-Denis
(p 90)

Best **French**
★★★ Toque!, $$$$$ 900 place
Jean-Paul-Riopelle (p 98)

Best **Fusion**
★ Chez l'Epicier, $$$ 331 rue
St-Paul est (p 92)

Best **Québécois**
★★ Aix Cuisine du Terroir, $$$$
711 Côte de la Place d'Armes (p 90)

*Previous page: A gourmet dish from
the kitchen of the Fairmont The Queen
Elizabeth hotel.*

Best **Service**
★★ Brunoise, $$$$ 3807 rue
St-Andre (p 91)

Best **Vegetarian**
Best **Traditional Poutine**
★ Casse-Croute La Banquise, $
994 rue Rachel est (p 91)

Best **Cheap Poutine**
Mamma's, $ 75 av. des Pins (p 95)

Best **Place to See and Be Seen**
Buona Notte, $$$–$$$$ 3518 bd.
St-Laurent (p 91)

Best **Charming Outdoor Dining**
★★ Les Remparts, $$$$ 93 rue de
la Commune (p 95)

*The Santropol cafe serves the best sand-
wiches in Montréal.*

Dining in the **Plateau**

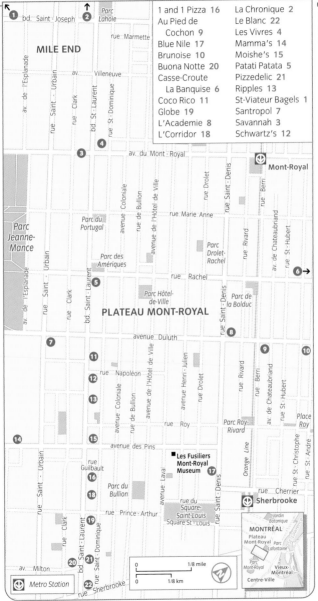

1 and 1 Pizza 16	La Chronique 2
Au Pied de Cochon 9	Le Blanc 22
Blue Nile 17	Les Vivres 4
Brunoise 10	Mamma's 14
Buona Notte 20	Moishe's 15
Casse-Croute La Banquise 6	Patati Patata 5
Coco Rico 11	Pizzedelic 21
Globe 19	Ripples 13
L'Academie 8	St-Viateur Bagels 1
L'Corridor 18	Santropol 7
	Savannah 3
	Schwartz's 12

MILE END

bd. Saint - Joseph

Parc Lahoie

rue Marmette

av. Villeneuve

av. de l'Esplanade

rue Saint - Urbain

rue Clark

bd. St-Laurent

rue St-Dominique

av. du Mont - Royal

Mont-Royal

Parc Jeanne-Mance

rue Drolet

rue Saint - Denis

rue Berri

av. de Chateaubriand

rue St - Hubert

Parc du Portugal

avenue Coloniale

rue de Bullion

avenue de l'Hôtel de Ville

rue Marie Anne

Parc des Amériques

rue Rachel

Parc Drolet-Rachel

rue Rivard

Parc Hôtel-de-Ville

PLATEAU MONT-ROYAL

Parc de la Bolduc

rue Saint - Denis

av. de l'Esplanade

rue Saint - Urbain

rue Clark

bd. Saint - Laurent

avenue Duluth

rue Napoléon

avenue Coloniale

rue de Bullion

avenue de l'Hôtel de Ville

avenue Henri - Julien

rue Drolet

rue Roy

rue Rivard

rue Berri

av. de Chateaubriand

rue St-Hubert

Parc Roy-Rivard

Place Roy

Orange Line

rue St-Christophe

rue St-André

avenue des Pins

rue Guilbault

Parc du Bullion

avenue Lava

■ **Les Fusiliers Mont-Royal Museum**

rue du *Square-Saint-Louis* Square St - Louis

rue Cherrier

Sherbrooke

rue Prince - Arthur

rue Saint - Denis

av. Milton

rue Saint - Urbain

rue Clark

bd. Saint-Laurent

rue Saint - Dominique

rue Sherbrooke

Metro Station

0   1/8 mile
0   1/8 km

Jardin Botanique

MONTRÉAL

Plateau Mont-Royal *Parc Lafontaine*

Parc Mont-Royal Vieux-Montréal

Centre-Ville

Dining in **Montréal**

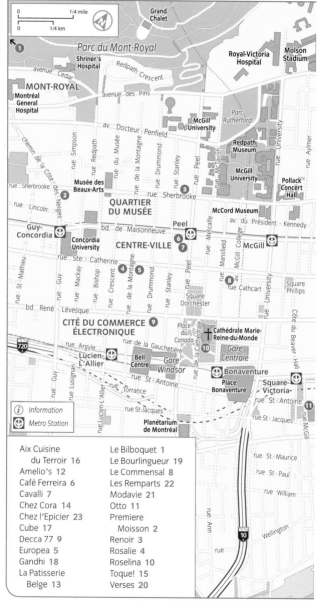

Aix Cuisine
   du Terroir 16
Amelio's 12
Café Ferreira 6
Cavalli 7
Chez Cora 14
Chez l'Epicier 23
Cube 17
Decca 77 9
Europea 5
Gandhi 18
La Patisserie
   Belge 13

Le Bilboquet 1
Le Bourlingueur 19
Le Commensal 8
Les Remparts 22
Modavie 21
Otto 11
Premiere
   Moisson 2
Renoir 3
Rosalie 4
Roselina 10
Toque! 15
Verses 20

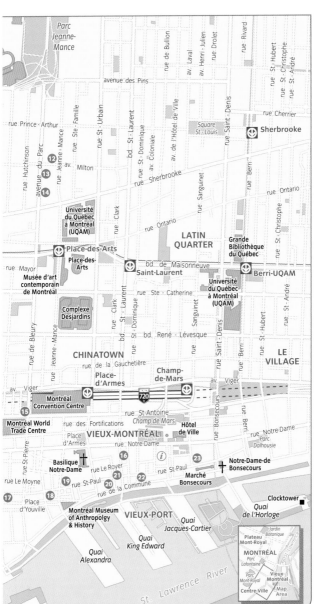

Restaurants A to Z

1 and 1 Pizza PLATEAU *PIZZA*
The only decent 99-cent pizza joint in a town where inexpensive pizza tastes cheap. After a night on the town on Boulevard St-Laurent, this small pizza parlor is strategically placed for a post-drinking, post-clubbing snack. *3679 bd. St-Laurent.* ☎ *514/982-0982. Most items under C$5. No credit cards. Lunch & dinner daily. Métro: St-Laurent. Map p 87.*

★★ Aix Cuisine du Terroir
VIEUX-MONTRÉAL *QUEBECOIS* The sophisticated flavors found in this restaurant's excellent regional preparations of fish, boar, and duck have justifiably garnered critical praise. Toss in the upscale decor and an intelligent waitstaff, and you have the ingredients for an exquisite dining experience. *711 Côte de la Place d'Armes (in the Hotel Place d'Armes).* ☎ *514/904-1201. www.aixcuisine.com. Main courses C$27–C$35. AE, DC, MC, V. Lunch & dinner Mon–Fri, dinner Sat–Sun. Métro: Place d'Armes. Map p 88.*

★ Amelio's
CENTRE-VILLE *ITALIAN* The only restaurant of note in the "McGill Ghetto" is this local favorite, a wonderful Italian bistro that serves an amazing five-cheese personal pizza and various pasta dishes. The intimate, homey surroundings and the ambient chatter makes you feel like you're eating with an extended family of 40. Bring your own wine. *201 rue Milton.* ☎ *514/845-8396. Most meals under C$15. No credit cards. Lunch & dinner daily. Map p 88.*

★★ Au Pied de Cochon
PLATEAU *QUEBECOIS* Some of the best meals at "The Pig's Foot" unsurprisingly feature different cuts of pork, though massive amounts of beef, chicken, lamb, duck, and venison are also used to create artery-clogging dishes that are sinfully delectable. Beware: This legendary place fills up extremely quickly during normal dining hours. ☎ *514/281-1116. Reservations strongly advised. Main courses C$12–C$35. MC, V. Dinner Tues–Sun. Métro: Sherbrooke. Map p 87.*

Blue Nile PLATEAU *ETHIOPIAN* Utensils are overrated. Ditch them and eat this popular restaurant's flavorful Ethiopian food with your hands. The aromatic meats are usually stewed or grilled and served on a large circular plate with stacks of warm, moist *injera*—a traditional Ethiopian bread. *3706 rue St-Denis.* ☎ *514/285-4628. Main courses C$15–C$30. AE, DC, MC, V. Dinner daily. Map p 87.*

For exceptional dining in Vieux-Montréal, head to Aix Cuisine du Terroir.

★★ **Brunoise** PLATEAU *FUSION*
This lovely bistro's experienced and amiable staff serves such globally influenced dishes as unbelievably tender veal cheeks with asparagus and pearl onions to a loyal crowd. It's an intimate but pricey dining treat. *3807 rue St-Andre.* ☎ *514/523-3885. Reservations recommended. Main courses C\$35–C\$46. AE, MC, V. Dinner daily. Closed 3 weeks at Christmas. Métro: Sherbrooke. Map p 87.*

★★ **Buona Notte** PLATEAU *ITAL-IAN* A favorite of celebrities (check out the collection of plates decorated by such celebrity diners as Celine Dion and Jim Carrey) and the Montréal Canadiens, Buona Notte sets the standard for posh St-Laurent restaurants. Others follow its formula: a distractingly gorgeous waitstaff, expensive gourmet food, and a clientele that's even more stunning than the employees. *3518 bd. St-Laurent.* ☎ *514/848-0644. www.buonanotte.com. Reservations recommended. Main courses C\$11–C\$40. AE, DC, MC, V. Lunch & dinner Mon–Sat, dinner Sun. Métro: St-Laurent. Map p 87.*

Café Ferreira CENTRE-VILLE *POR-TUGUESE* The food is excellent, but patrons are more impressed by this popular downtown restaurant's decor than the succulent Portuguese lamb chops over which it prides itself. The gold and blue color scheme, along with a smattering of art, makes for a very relaxing dinner experience. *1446 rue Peel.* ☎ *514/848-0988. www.ferreiracafe.com. Reservations recommended. Main courses C\$27–C\$89. MC, V. Lunch & dinner Mon–Fri; dinner only Sat. Métro: Peel. Map p 88.*

★ **Casse-Croute La Banquise** PLATEAU *LIGHT FARE* Quebecois love this place not for its fast food, but for the best poutine east of the Plateau. Never scrimping on ingredients, the chefs use real cheese curds

The upscale dishes at Buona Notte attract a very hip clientele.

instead of regular cheese, and the gravy is among the tastiest in town. *994 rue Rachel Est.* ☎ *514/525-2415. No credit cards. C\$4–C\$6. Open 24 hr. daily. Map p 87.*

Cavalli CENTRE-VILLE *ITALIAN* Like many joints on St-Laurent, Cavalli relies on good looks for business: The staff and the bartenders behind the pink bar are picked more for their perfect bone structure than their actual skills, and the gorgeous clientele are strategically seated streetside. The food, however, is excellent, and the linguine and scallops get high marks. *2040 rue Peel.* ☎ *514/843-5100. Reservations recommended. Main courses C\$30–C\$40. AE, MC, V. Mon–Fri 11:30am–3pm and 5:30–10:30pm; Sat–Sun 5:30–10:30pm (bar open later). Métro: Peel. Map p 88.*

★ **Chez Cora** CENTRE-VILLE *LIGHT FARE* The tasty omelets and crepes at this small chain of breakfast bistros are a great way to start any day. Order the Special Cora (a combination of sausage, bacon, eggs, home fries, and a crepe) and an endless cup of coffee, and you'll have enough energy to hop every set of stairs on Mont-Royal. *3465 av. du Parc.* ☎ *514/849-4932. www.chezcora.com. Most meals under C\$15. AE, MC, V. Breakfast & lunch daily. Map p 88.*

Chez l'Epicier is one of the best places in the city for innovative comfort food.

★ **Chez l'Epicier** VIEUX-MON-TREAL *FUSION* For an interesting combination of innovation and comfort food, head to this atmospheric haunt, one of Montréal's most inventive and original restaurants. It's frequented by diners looking for international twists on familiar French dishes, such as rösti made of sweet potato and Asian spices. Don't leave without sampling the decadent dessert menu. *331 rue St-Paul est.* ☎ *514/878-2232. Main courses C$20–C$38. AE, DC, DISC, MC, V. Lunch & dinner Mon–Fri, dinner Sat–Sun. Métro: Champ-de-Mars. Map p 88.*

Coco Rico PLATEAU *FAST FOOD* An inexpensive and popular local favorite, Coco Rico cooks up wonderfully seasoned Portuguese rotisserie chicken for folks on the go.

Tack on some egg-sized potatoes and tasty cornbread and you'll have enough food for a personal banquet. *3907 bd. St-Laurent.* ☎ *514/ 849-5554. Most items under C$12. No credit cards. Lunch & dinner daily. Map p 87.*

★ **Cube** VIEUX-MONTREAL *FUSION* This chic and urbane hotel restaurant serves up stylish dishes that are easy on the eyes and a treat for the stomach. You'll find high-class staples such as foie gras at dinner, but the true gem is the lunch menu's sumptuous roasted Cornish hen, stuffed with sauerkraut and asparagus. *355 rue McGill (inside the Hôtel St-Paul).* ☎ *514/876-2823. Reservations recommended. Main courses C$30–C$42. AE, DC, MC, V. Lunch & dinner daily. Métro: Square Victoria. Map p 88.*

Decca 77 CENTRE-VILLE *INTERNA-TIONAL* A relatively strange mix of business execs, concert-goers, and hockey fans (from the nearby Bell Centre) dine at this stylish restaurant, which doesn't care if patrons wear a three-piece suit or a Koivu jersey. Highlights include the delicious tandoori rack of lamb and the juicy buffalo tenderloin. *1077 rue Drummond.* ☎ *514/934-1077. www. decca77.com. Main courses C$25– C$40. AE, DC, MC, V. Lunch & dinner Mon–Fri, dinner Sat. Map p 88.*

The popular L'Academie is the city's top BYOB restaurant. See p. 94.

Cabanes au Sucre

Throughout Canada's history maple syrup has been an economic and cultural boon for Québecers. Once the snows thaw, the thick, brown liquid is harvested from the numerous maple forests south of Montréal. Locals often bear witness to the entire process by visiting the *cabanes au sucre* or "sugar shacks," where the syrup is refined and bottled. These shacks also serve up meals that contain generous helpings of the sugary ingredient and, if they haven't had their fill yet, visitors can take part in the age-old tradition of *"tire sur la neige."* Fresh, hot maple syrup is brought out into the open and poured onto a clean layer of snow; then you pick up the semi-soft confection before it hardens and enjoy what's known as "maple toffee." If you don't want to schlep out of town, you'll find plenty of dishes in Montréal restaurants that feature the sweet syrup.

Europea CENTRE-VILLE *FRENCH/MEDITERRANEAN* Securing a table at this cozy restaurant (seating only about 30), can be difficult, but chef Jerome Ferrer's sumptuous *foie gras de canard au torchon* (a delicious duck foie gras dish) is worth the effort and the C$22 price tag. For something a little more substantial, the Chilean sea bass is an excellent and delicious alternative. *1227 rue de la Montagne. 514/398-9229. Reservations strongly recommended. C$22–C$40. AE, DC, MC, V. Lunch & dinner Mon–Fri; dinner Sat–Sun. Métro: Peel. Map p 88.*

★ **Gandhi** VIEUX-MONTREAL*INDIAN* The always busy but wonderfully cozy Gandhi won't disappoint with its usual Indian fare (chicken tandoori, tikka, and so on), but it's the little twists on their interesting curries that will leave your taste buds tingling. *230 rue St-Paul.* ☎ *514/845-5866. Reservations recommended on weekends.*

Main courses C$15–C$30. Lunch & dinner daily. Métro: Place d'Armes. Map p 88.

★ **Globe** PLATEAU *CONTEMPORARY ITALIAN* The waitstaff and clientele, in true St-Laurent style, are all eye-candy for the executives that frequent this pricey but trendy spot. The great food on the ever-changing menu keeps the critics happy. *3455 bd. St-Laurent.* ☎ *514/284-3823. Reservations suggested. Main courses C$30–C$50. AE, DC, MC, V. Dinner daily. Métro: St-Laurent. Map p 87.*

★ **L'Academie** PLATEAU *MEDITERRANEAN* The top "Bring Your Own Wine" destination on St-Denis has a modern, upscale decor, but those in casual wear won't feel out of place. Grab a bottle from the SAQ conveniently located next door and order one of the excellent pasta dishes. Or try one of the enjoyable though not always filling *moule et frites*

The region's delicious maple syrup is a widely used ingredient in Montréal's restaurants.

The Best Dining

(mussels and fries) options. *4051 rue St-Denis.* ☎ *514/849-2249. Main courses C$12–C$28. AE, DC, MC, V. Lunch & dinner daily. Map p 87.*

L'Corridor PLATEAU *CARIBBEAN* The perfectly marinated jerk chicken at this Caribbean eatery is top-notch, jumping with flavor and spice. Wash it down with the refreshing ginger beer for an inexpensive but satisfying meal. *3655 bd. St-Laurent. 514/350-5320. No credit cards. C$8–C$16. Lunch (after 2pm) & dinner daily. Map p 88.*

★★ La Chronique MILE END *FUSION* Its simple but attractive decor might suggest otherwise, but La Chronique's exquisitely prepared meals are proof that it's one of the top restaurants in the city. The fusion bistro produces a mouthwatering combination of duck and roasted shrimps with caviar d'aubergines and portabella mushrooms. A must if you're in the area. *99 rue Laurier.* ☎ *514/271-4770. www.lachronique. qc.ca. Reservations required. Main courses C$28–C$36. AE, DC, MC, V. Lunch & dinner Tues–Fri, dinner Sat. Closed first 2 weeks of July. Métro: Laurier. Map p 87.*

The chic Le Blanc is a hotspot for fusion cuisine.

La Patisserie Belge CENTRE-VILLE *BAKERY* La Patisserie Belge is perfectly good for bakery basics, but its best for its mouthwatering quiches, whose soft, flaky crusts and luscious fillings make a visit here worth the walk. *3485 av. du Parc.* ☎ *514/845-1245. www.lapatisseriebelge.com. Most items under C$12. AE, MC, V. Breakfast & lunch daily. Métro: Place des Arts. Map p 88.*

kids Le Bilboquet OUTREMONT *ICE CREAM* When the mercury hits 90°F (32°C) degrees, Montréalers cool off at this little spot on trendy rue Bernard. The ice cream, churned in-house, is served in generous portions and comes in such mouthwatering flavors as maple taffy and white chocolate cashew. *1311 rue Bernard ouest.* ☎ *514/ 276-0414. Most items under C$8. No credit cards. Open daily. Map p 88.*

A sorbet "cake" is just one of the frosty treat you can order at Le Bilboquet.

★ Le Blanc PLATEAU *FUSION* Whether you choose a cozy booth in the back or a window seat to watch the parade of Montréalers on St-Laurent, you'll be pleasantly surprised with Le Blanc's take on traditional Italian and French dishes. Ostrich, duck, and pigeon are just some of the meats used in this chic hot spot's gourmet creations. *3435 bd. St-Laurent.* ☎ *514/288-9909. Reservations suggested. Main courses C$30–C$45. AE, DC, MC, V. Lunch & dinner Mon–Fri, dinner Sat–Sun. Métro: Sherbrooke. Map p 87.*

Le Bourlingueur VIEUX-MON-TREAL *FRENCH* It may look slightly out of place among the quaint-chic places in Old Montréal, but don't let the bucolic furnishings deter you. Relax in the restaurant's warm, homey ambience as you dine on one of the amazing (and well-priced) meals offered on their chalkboard menu—such as the succulent roasted pork with apple sauces. *363 rue St-Francois-Xavier.* ☎ *514/845-3646. Reservations recommended on weekends. Main courses C$10–C$18. MC, V. Lunch & dinner daily. Métro: Place d'Armes. Map p 88.*

Le Commensal CENTRE-VILLE *VEGETARIAN* Choose from a huge selection of hot and cold dishes at this buffet-style vegetarian restaurant, then pile as much as you want on your plate. Despite the cafeteria feel, the presentation and flavor of the food still manages to be tasteful and tasty. *1204 av. McGill College.* ☎ *514/871-1480. Most meals under C$12. AE, MC, V. Lunch & dinner daily. Métro: McGill or Bonaventure. Map p 88.*

★★ Les Remparts VIEUX MON-TRÉAL *FRENCH* Dine on amazingly prepared French cuisine in the main ground-floor dining room, or get treated to one of the best rooftop dining terraces in Old Montréal (though with a more limited menu). You can't go wrong with the expertly served savory snapper or butter-roasted venison. *93 rue de la Commune.* ☎ *514/392-1649. www. restaurantlesremparts.com. Reservations recommended. Main courses C$30–C$40. Lunch & dinner Mon–Fri, dinner Sat–Sun. Métro: Place D'Armes. Map p 88.*

★★ Les Vivres PLATEAU *VEGAN* Carnivores won't notice that the fresh and tasty dishes are missing meat (and all other animal products). The miso-potato soup, prepared

For topnotch French cuisine and great outdoor dining, head to Les Remparts.

ever-so-carefully by the co-operative running the restaurant, is always seasoned perfectly. *4631 bd. St-Laurent.* ☎ *514/842-3479. Most meals under C$15. No credit cards. Lunch & dinner daily. Map p 87.*

Mamma's PLATEAU *LIGHT FARE* Another poutine favorite, though not for traditionalists (who cringe at the lack of cheese curds). Around since 1966, the conveniently located Mamma's stays open late and serves mostly diner food, but most come for the large, gooey plates of fries, gravy, and melted cheese. *75 av. des Pins.* ☎ *514/288-1128. Most meals under C$15. MC, V. Lunch & dinner daily. Map p 87. Métro: Sherbrooke.*

★ Modavie VIEUX-MONTREAL *MEDITERRANEAN* The steaks and fish dishes are exemplary, but for a real treat try the delightful lamb duo. A live jazz band performs every night, but what's on your plate and in your glass (the wine list is extensive) will truly command your attention. *1 rue St-Paul.* ☎ *514/287-9582. www.modavie.com. Reservations recommended. Main courses C$15–C$35. AE, DC, MC, V. Lunch & dinner*

Montreal's restaurants are notable for their vast array of cheese selections; be sure to sample a few when dining out.

Say Cheese

When dining in Montréal, do yourself a favor and be sure to sample one of the many varieties of cheese (over 300 of them) served in the city's restaurants. The cheeses of Québec are renowned for their rich flavors and textures, and most of them can't be sampled outside of Canada because they're made from unpasteurized milk. Just some of the many notable choices include the citrus-flavored Cantonnier; the buttery St-Basil de Port Neuf; the Gruyère-like Le Moine; the rich and creamy Blue Ermite; the semi-soft Le Migneron (made from goat's milk); the Brie-style Belle Creame; and Chèvre Noire, a sharp goats-milk variety that's covered in black wax.

daily. Métro: Place d'Armes. Map p 88.

★★ **Moishe's** PLATEAU *STEAK-HOUSE* The city's best steakhouse has been frequented by celebrities and politicians since it opened in 1938. The top sirloin is meticulously prepared and cooked, resulting in the most tender and succulent slice of red meat north of the border. *3961 bd. St-Laurent.* ☎ *514/845-3509. Reservations recommended. Main courses C$26–C$46. AE, DC, MC, V. Lunch & dinner Mon–Fri. Métro: Sherbrooke. Map p 87.*

Moishe's is Montréal's premiere steakhouse.

Otto VIEUX-MONTRÉAL *ITALIAN/ MEDITERRANEAN* The W Hotel's official (though unpretentious) restaurant specializes in dishes that are heavy on the calamari, crab, fish, and shrimp— arguably the best seafood in town. There are non-marine alternatives for landlubbers. *901 Square Victoria (in the W Hotel).* ☎ *514/395-3183. Reservations recommended. Main courses C$30– C$45. Lunch & dinner daily. Métro: Square Victoria. Map p 88.*

★ **Patati Patata** PLATEAU *DINER* Unless you're dining alone, plan on getting takeout from this friendly nook, which seats no more than a dozen patrons at a time. The breakfasts and burgers are top-notch, as is the award-worthy poutine. *4177 bd. St-Laurent.* ☎ *514/844-0216. Most items under C$7. No credit cards. Breakfast, lunch & dinner daily. Map p 87.*

kids **Pizzedelic** PLATEAU *PIZZA* Thanks to ingredients such as filet mignon, apple, and cumin, this is not your typical pizza. The quirky combinations at this fork-and-knife joint are both interesting and delectable. *3509 bd. St-Laurent.* ☎ *514/282-6784. Pizzas and main courses C$11–C$20. AE, DC, MC, V. Lunch & dinner daily. Métro: St-Laurent. Map p 87.*

★ Premiere Moisson

CENTRE-VILLE *BAKERY*
Montréal's best bakery (there are multiple branches scattered throughout the city) got its reputation by pulling wonderful loaves of sweet bread and baguettes (over 40 varieties) out of its ovens. It's perfect for picnic fare. *1490 rue Sherbrooke ouest.* ☎ *514/931-6540. www.premiere moisson.com. Most items under C$12. MC, V. Breakfast, lunch & dinner daily. Map p 88.*

Premiere Moisson sells more than 40 varieties of bread and is one of the best spots in town for picnic supplies.

Renoir CENTRE-VILLE *FUSION*

Executives love to spend their lunch hour savoring the flavorful, creative, and mostly French cuisine at this swank hotel restaurant. For quieter dining, come here for dinner. *1155 rue Sherbrooke ouest (in the Sofitel Hotel).* ☎ *514/285-9000. Reservations suggested. Main courses C$20–C$35. AE, DC, DISC, MC, V. Breakfast, lunch & dinner daily. Map p 88.*

Ripples PLATEAU *ICE CREAM*

This ice cream hot spot's chocolate version has many French-Canadian fans: Locals swear this is the only place to go for a scoop of the sweet brown frozen treat. The other flavors, such as guava-pineapple or ginger, are just as tasty. *3880 bd. St-Laurent.* ☎ *514/842-1697. Most items under C$4. No credit cards. Open daily. Map p 87.*

Rosalie CENTRE-VILLE *CONTEMPO-RARY FRENCH*

An extraordinarily beautiful staff waits hand and foot on the incredibly successful clientele that enjoys this upscale restaurant's tasty cuisine. Diners can do no wrong by ordering the always delicious fish of the day. *1232 rue de la Montagne.* ☎ *514/392-1970. Reservations recommended. Main courses C$20–C$40. AE, DC, MC, V. Lunch & dinner Mon–Fri; dinner Sat–Sun. Métro: Peel. Map p 87.*

Roselina CENTRE-VILLE *ITALIAN*

Its convenient location on the ground floor of Montréal's tallest skyscraper makes Roselina a decent option after a skating session at the Underground City's rink, but the Italian dishes fall somewhat short of stellar. *1000 rue de la Gauchetiere.* ☎ *514/876-4343. Main courses C$14–C$22. AE, MC, V. Lunch & dinner daily. Map p 88.*

★ Santropol PLATEAU *FUSION/SANDWICH*

Students and locals love this sandwich spot on the corner of Duluth and St. Urbain. The eccentric, yet homey, interior somehow reflects the curious combination of ingredients found in its sandwiches. Piled between the slices of rye or pumpernickel are an odd assortment of vegetables, meats and spreads that will easily satisfy the hungriest of diners. *3990 rue St-Urbain.* ☎ *514/842-3110. www.santropol.com. Main courses C$7–C$10. No credit cards. Lunch & dinner daily. Métro: Mont-Royal. Map p. 87.*

Pizzedelic is noted for its quirky toppings and delicious pizzas.

The legendary Schwartz's is renowned for its smoked meat.

★★ Savannah PLATEAU *FUSION*
This critically acclaimed "Southern fusion" restaurant showcases Cajun, creole, and other Southern styles. Dine indoors or out on such treats as scrumptious crab cakes with andouille sausage. *4448 bd. St-Laurent.* ☎ *514/904-0277. Main courses C$18–C$32. Breakfast, lunch & dinner daily. Reservations recommended. AE, DC, MC, V. Map p 87.*

★★★ Schwartz's PLATEAU *DELI*
This legendary Montréal eatery is crowded, waiters are brusque, the counter can get dirty, and the line can reach the end of the block. Despite all of this, I'd fight to the death just to get a taste of the savory meat, the salty side of pickles and fries, and a can of syrupy Cott's black cherry soda. *3895 bd. St-Laurent.* ☎ *514/842-4813. Main courses C$6–C$14. No credit cards. Breakfast, lunch & dinner daily. Métro: St-Laurent. Map p 87.*

★★★ Toque! CENTRE-VILLE
FRENCH/FUSION The celebrated Toque! overwhelms with unparalleled service and dazzling cuisine (and the bill). Opt for one of the tasting menus to ease the decision-making process and to better sample the famed kitchen's amazing creations. *900 place Jean-Paul-Riopelle.*

☎ *514/499-2084. www.restaurant-toque.com. Reservations required. Main courses C$31–C$45; degustation menus C$88–C$98. AE, MC, V. Lunch & dinner Tues–Fri, dinner Sat. Closed Dec 24–Jan 6. Métro: Sherbrooke. Map p 88.*

★★★ St-Viateur Bagels MILE
END *BAKERY* Famous around the world for their dense, sweet dough, Montréal's oven-fired bagels have gained most of their renown through St-Viateur's. This small shop in the Plateau has been boiling bagels in honeyed water and baking them for years. Don't leave the city without sampling a few straight from the oven. *1127 av. Mont Royal.* ☎ *514/528-6361. www.stviateur bagel.com. Most items under C$10, individual bagels 60¢ each. No credit cards. Open 24 hr. daily. Métro: Mont Royal. Map p 87.*

★★ Verses VIEUX-MONTREAL
FRENCH Verses is one of the few places in Old Montréal that boasts an outdoor dining terrace. The outdoor menu is more limited than the one in the main ground-floor restaurant, where you can sink your teeth into expertly cooked venison. *106 rue St-Paul.* ☎ *514/842-1887. Reservations recommended. Main courses C$28–C$41. AE, DC, MC, V. Breakfast, lunch & dinner daily. Métro: Square Victoria. Map p 88.* ●

Savor expertly prepared cuisine, indoors or out, at Verses in Vieux-Montréal.

Nightlife Best Bets

Best Singles' Scene
★ Sir Winston Churchill Pub Complex, *1459 rue Crescent (p 108)*

Best Kitsch
★ Copacobana, *3910 bd. St-Laurent (p 106)*

Best Place to Spot a Local Celebrity
★ Buona Notte, *3518 bd. St-Laurent (p 106)*

Best Place for People-Watching
★★★ Bar St-Sulpice, *1680 rue St-Denis (p 105)*

Best Beers
★ Brutopia, *1219 rue Crescent (p 105)*

Best View
Altitude 737, *1 place Ville Marie (p 109)*

Best Irish Pub
★★ Hurley's, *1225 rue Crescent (p 106)*

Best Bar to Watch the Habs Play
Le Cage Aux Sports, *1437 bd. Rene Levesque ouest (p 107)*

Best Rock Bar
★ Les Foufounes Electrique, *87 rue Ste-Catherine oest (p 107)*

Best Sports Bar
Champs, *3956 bd. St-Laurent (p 106)*

Best DJ
Blue Dog, *3958 bd. St-Laurent (p 105)*

Best Lounge
★★ Lola Lounge, *1023 rue de Bleury (p 107)*

Best Dive Bar
★ Biftek, *3702 bd. St-Laurent (p 105)* and ★ Copacobana, *3910 bd. St-Laurent (p 106)*

Previous page: Musicians play at Montréal's famed International Festival of Jazz.

La Cage Aux Sports, the best bar in town for watching a Canadiens game.

Best for Romance
★★ Le Sainte Élisabeth Pub European, *1412 rue St-Elisabeth (p 107)*

Best Bartenders
★ Brutopia, *1219 rue Crescent (p 105)*

Best Bar for Twenty-somethings
★★ Le Pistol, *3723 bd. St-Laurent (p 107)*

Best Bar for Cigar Aficionados
Stogies, *2015 rue Crescent (p 108)*

Best for Beer and Breakfast
Shed Café, *3515 bd. St-Laurent (p 108)*

Best Find
★★ Le Sainte Elisabeth Pub European, *1412 rue St-Elisabeth (p 107)*

Best Club for Reliving the '60s
Go Go Lounge, *3682 bd. St-Laurent (p 106)*

Best Club for Reliving the '70s
Funkytown, *1454 rue Peel (p 109)*

Best Gay Bar
★★ Le Drugstore, *1360 rue Ste-Catherine est (p 110)*

Best Dance Club
★★★ Tokyo Bar, *3709 bd. St-Laurent (p 110)*

Best After-Hours Club
★ Stereo, *858 rue Ste-Catherine est (p 110)*

Nightlife in the Plateau

Barfly 1
Bar St-Sulpice 17
Biftek 9
Blue Dog 3
Buona Notte 16
Café Campus 13
Champs 4
Copacobana 5
Frappe 6
Go-Go Lounge 11
Jupiter Room 7
L'Barouf 2
Le Parking 21
Le Pistol 10
Le Sainte Élisabeth
   Pub European 19
Les Foufounes
   Electrique 18
Orchid 14
Roy Bar 8
Shed Café 15
Stereo 20
Tokyo Bar 12

Nightlife in Centre-Ville

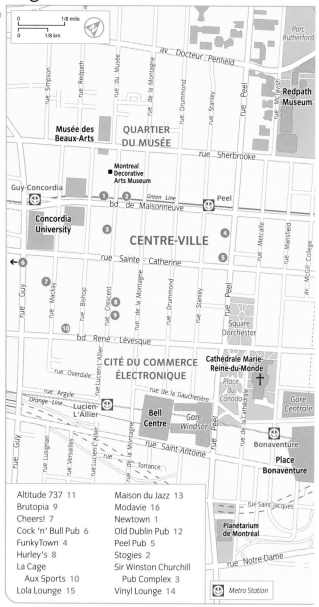

0   1/8 mile
0   1/8 km

Parc Rutherford

av. Docteur-Penfield

rue Simpson
rue Redpath
rue du Musée
rue de la Montagne
rue Drummond
rue Stanley
rue Peel
rue McTavish

Redpath Museum

Musée des Beaux-Arts

QUARTIER DU MUSÉE

rue Sherbrooke

Montreal Decorative Arts Museum

Guy-Concordia

Green Line

bd. de Maisonneuve

Peel

Concordia University

CENTRE-VILLE

rue Metcalfe
rue Mansfield

rue Sainte-Catherine

av. McGill College

rue Guy
rue Mackay
rue Bishop
rue Crescent
rue de la Montagne
rue Drummond
rue Stanley
rue Peel

Square Dorchester

bd. René-Lévesque

rue Lucien-L'Allier

rue Overdale

CITÉ DU COMMERCE ÉLECTRONIQUE

Cathédrale Marie-Reine-du-Monde

Place du Canada

rue Argyle

Orange Line

Lucien-L'Allier

rue de la Gauchetière

Gare Centrale

rue Guy
rue Lusignan
rue Versailles
rue Lucien-L'Allier

Bell Centre

Gare Windsor

rue de la Montagne

rue Peel

rue de la Cathédrale

rue Saint-Antoine

Bonaventure

Place Bonaventure

rue de Torrance

rue Saint-Jacques

Planétarium de Montréal

rue Notre-Dame

Altitude 737 **11**	Maison du Jazz **13**
Brutopia **9**	Modavie **16**
Cheers! **7**	Newtown **1**
Cock 'n' Bull Pub **6**	Old Dublin Pub **12**
FunkyTown **4**	Peel Pub **5**
Hurley's **8**	Stogies **2**
La Cage	Sir Winston Churchill
Aux Sports **10**	Pub Complex **3**
Lola Lounge **15**	Vinyl Lounge **14**

Metro Station

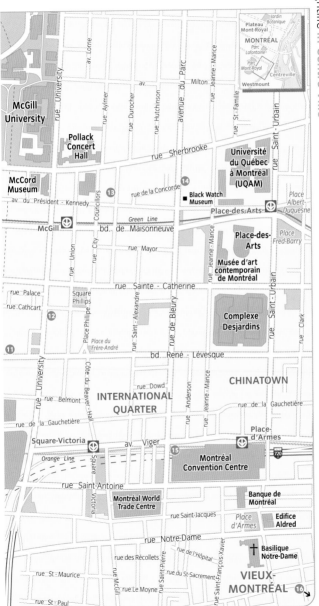

Nightlife in Northeast Montréal

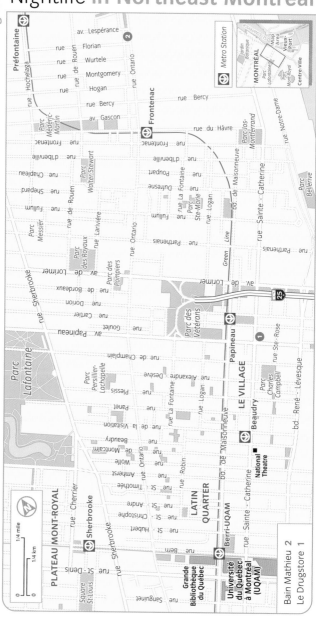

Préfontaine

av. Lespérance

rue Florian
rue Wurtele
rue Montgomery
rue Hogan

rue de Rouen
rue Hochelaga

rue Bercy
av. Gascon

Parc Médéric-Martin

rue Ontario

rue Frontenac

Frontenac

rue Bercy

rue du Hâvre

rue Frontenac

rue d'Iberville
rue d'Iberville

rue Chapleau
rue Shepard
rue Fullum

Parc Walter-Stewart

Poupart
Dufresne
rue Fullum

rue

Parc Messier

rue de Rouen
rue Larivière
rue Lanoraie

Parc La Fontaine
Parc Ste-Marie

rue Logan

bd. de Maisonneuve

Parc Jos-Montferrand

rue Notre-Dame

Parc BelRive

rue Sainte - Catherine

Parc des Royaux
Parc des Pompiers

rue Ontario
rue Parthenais

Green Line

rue Parthenais

rue de Bordeaux

av. de Lormier

av. de Lormier

rue Sherbrooke

rue Cartier
rue Dorion
rue Goulet

Parc des Vétérans

25

av. Papineau

rue de Champlain

Papineau

rue Ste-Rose

LE VILLAGE

Parc Lafontaine

Parc Persillier-Lachapelle

rue Alexandre - Desève

rue Logan

Parc Charles Campbell

rue Plessis
rue Panet
rue de la Visitation

rue La Fontaine

bd. René - Lévesque

Beaudry

rue Beaudry
rue de Montcalm
rue Wolfe
rue Amherst
rue St - Timothée
rue St - André
rue St - Christophe
rue St - Hubert
rue Berri

rue Robin

rue Ontario

bd. de Maisonneuve

National Theatre

rue Sainte - Catherine

Berri-UQAM

LATIN QUARTER

Sherbrooke

rue Cherrier

rue Sherbrooke

PLATEAU MONT-ROYAL

Square St-Louis
rue St-Denis
rue Sanguinet

Grande Bibliothèque du Québec

Université du Québec à Montréal (UQAM)

Metro Station

Jardin Botanique

Parc Lafontaine

MONTRÉAL

Parc Mont-Royal

Centre-Ville

Vieux Port

Map Area

1/4 mile
1/4 km

Bain Mathieu 2
Le Drugstore 1

Montréal Nightlife A to Z

Bars and Cafes

Bain Mathieu FRONTENAC   Also the site of infinitheatre's (p 115) performances, the empty pool at Bain Mathieu is a popular watering hole for locals, particularly artists. An easygoing crowd mingles over mixed drinks and cocktails at the tables set up near the deep end—definitely a unique experience. *2915 rue Ontario est.* ☎ *514/523-3265. Métro: Frontenac.*

Barfly PLATEAU   Half-bar/half concert venue, Barfly draws an interesting group of punky university students to its tiny confines. There's usually a rock, punk or blues show staged once a week; at other times, the somewhat ratty bar serves up a rip-roaring, beer-guzzling good time to its college-age patrons. *4062a bd. St-Laurent.* ☎ *514/284-6665. Métro: Mont-Royal. Map p 101.*

★★★ **Bar St-Sulpice** QUARTIER LATIN   This four-story and immensely popular bar (the Montréal version of a Munich beer garden) is set in a converted mansion that has a bookshelf-laden alcove, a streetside terrace, a pool table area, and dance floors on both the top floor and basement. In summer and on warm spring nights, the gigantic outdoor terrace in the back is one of the busiest and noisiest places on St-Denis. *1680 rue St-Denis.* ☎ *514/844-9458. Métro: Berri-UQAM. Map p 101.*

★ **Biftek** PLATEAU   Despite new anti-smoking laws, the first floor of Montréal's best dive bar (and my favorite in the city) can get extremely smoky. Retreat to the second level where a conversation can be had and pool can be played—all while listening to the city's best rotation of indie and classic rock (with some good '80s tunes thrown in for posterity). *3702 bd. St-Laurent.* ☎ *514/844-6211. Métro: Sherbrooke or St-Laurent. Map p 101.*

Blue Dog PLATEAU   The tiny Blue Dog features some of the most talented DJs in town, and when there's enough room it's an extremely fun dance haunt (though it's usually packed). A few seats and a worn-out couch give the funky, college-age patrons a perch from which to enjoy whoever's behind the turntables. *3958 bd. St-Laurent.* ☎ *514/848-7006. Métro: St-Laurent. Map p 101.*

★ **Brutopia** CENTRE-VILLE   Beer aficionados will quickly befriend the barkeep, who pours everything from Québec microbrews to Indian pale ales to the bar's own homebrewed beer. The honey brown is particularly tasty and refreshing. *1219 rue Crescent.* ☎ *514/393-9277. www. brutopia.net. Métro: Lucien L'Allier. Map p 102.*

Buona Notte's bar attracts Montréal's hippest after-dark crowd. See p. 106.

★ **Buona Notte** PLATEAU   A top-notch restaurant (p 91), but as the night rolls on and the music gets louder, the impossibly attractive clientele shifts closer to the bar and closer to each other. Sport your finest threads or you won't catch even a passing glance. *3518 bd. St-Laurent.* ☎ *514/848-0644. Métro: St-Laurent. Map p 101.*

Champs PLATEAU   The best place to catch a major sporting event, this often-packed bar has flatscreen TVs everywhere so you don't miss any action. Settle with your buddies in a booth for sports-friendly (and rather expensive) munchies and pints of Molson. *3956 bd. St-Laurent.* ☎ *514/987-6444. www.champssportsbar.ca. Métro: Mont Royal. Map p 101.*

Cheers! CENTRE-VILLE   Ladies' night is when this meet-market for young singles is at its busiest. Top-40 hits are piped through the sprawling space of this bar/pub while the crowd works their mojo. *1260 rue Mackay.* ☎ *514/932-3138. www.cheersbars.com Cover free–C$6. Métro: Guy-Concordia. Map p 102.*

★ **Copacobana** PLATEAU   Tropical decorations don't seem to affect the young, laid-back crowd at this kitschy and unpretentious dive bar. Naturally, it's a hot spot for the Montréal college crowd. *3910 bd. St-Laurent.* ☎ *514/982-0800. Métro: Sherbrooke. Map p 101.*

★ **Cock 'n' Bull Pub** CENTRE-VILLE   You can't go wrong mixing collages and alcohol at this fun little bar, to which the city's twentysomethings flock for its Arts and Crafts nights and surprisingly decent bar food. Unpretentious and cheap, it's a dive bar worth visiting. *1944 rue Ste-Catherine ouest.* ☎ *514/933-4556. Métro: Guy-Concordia. Map p 102.*

A college-age crowd loves to rack up a few games at Copacabana.

Frappe PLATEAU   This bar's no-frills approach, in combination with its sheer size (you'll always find a free table), make it a hit with students and locals alike. In addition to its great happy-hour deals, you'll find a number of pool tables, foosball tables, TVs, and a decent terrace. *3900 bd. St-Laurent.* ☎ *514/289-9462. Métro: Sherbrooke. Map p 101.*

Go-Go Lounge PLATEAU   Even in the blistering cold of winter there's always a line to get inside this cramped place, but its fans brave frostbite and dress in retro-chic '60s threads as they mingle with other "swingers" among the psychedelic joint's bubble chairs and lava lamps. It's a great time in the warmer months, but not worth the numb extremities in winter. *3682 bd. St-Laurent.* ☎ *514/286-0882. Métro: St-Laurent. Map p 101.*

★★ **Hurley's** CENTRE-VILLE   This festive Irish pub is one of the few nightspots where you'll see college kids, middle-aged folks, and retirees sharing a pint. The former go through their ale at a quicker rate than the latter, but everyone enjoys the live Irish music that's played on most nights. *1225 rue Crescent.* ☎ *514/861-4111. www.hurleysirishpub.com. Métro: Peel or Guy-Concordia. Map p 102.*

L'Barouf PLATEAU   People (usually in groups) come here to take part in, or watch people take part in, the consumption of this rowdy bar's gimmicky "tower" of beer, which holds 6 liters of ale. The vertically impressive plastic tube (so drinkers can watch their progress) features its own mini-tap at the bottom. *4171 rue St-Denis.* ☎ *514/844-0119. Métro: Mont Royal. Map p 101.*

La Cage Aux Sports CENTRE-VILLE   If you couldn't score tickets to a Habs game, watch it at this sports bar, which is home to some of the rowdiest Canadiens fans around. During the hockey season, you'll find yourself surrounded by a sea of red, white, and blue jerseys. *1437 bd. Rene Levesque ouest.* ☎ *514/878-2243. www.cage.ca. Métro: Bonaventure. Map p 102.*

★★ **Le Pistol** PLATEAU   The young-un's love this über-trendy bar. It's hard to fault Le Pistol, with its great music satellite TVs and slinky decor, but there's an air of pretentiousness that's especially palpable when local indie music big shots The Stills and Sam Roberts (both friends of the management) take their booth in the back. *3723 bd. St-Laurent.* ☎ *514/847-2222. Métro: Sherbrooke. Map p 101.*

★★ **Le Sainte Élisabeth Pub European** QUARTIER LATIN   This small and popular publike bar has one of the best outdoor terraces in town—three surrounding walls, covered in ivy, stretch high into the Montréal sky as strategically placed lights make you forget you're anywhere close to an unsavory part of rue Ste-Catherine. It's open even in the winter, when scattered heat lamps keep patrons warm as they down one of several imported beers. *1412 rue Ste-Elisabeth.* ☎ *514/286-4302. www.ste-elisabeth.com. Métro: Berri-UQAM. Map p 101.*

★ **Les Foufounes Electrique** QUARTIER LATIN   It may have lost its edge in recent years, but "The Electric Buttocks" is a city landmark for unabashed rock music (hard rock and industrial bands love to play here) and a cold mug of beer. The area around this massive club/bar can be a little suspect, but the punk kids that hang on the street are harmless. *87 rue Ste-Catherine oest.* ☎ *514/844-5539. www.foufounes.qc.ca. Cover free–C$15. Métro: Berri-UQAM. Map p 101.*

★★ **Lola Lounge** CENTRE-VILLE A twenty-something crowd comes here for tasty amaretto sours and the excellent hip-hop/R&B that spins on a nightly basis. The lounge has a laid-back ambience and semi-antique couches, and boasts a good deal of breathing room. *1023 rue de Bleury.* ☎ *514/875-0004. Cover free–C$5. Métro: Place-des-Arts. Map p 102.*

★★★ **Maison du Jazz** CENTRE-VILLE   The legendary "Biddles" has dropped the name of famous Montréal jazz musician Charlie Biddles altogether, but luckily not much else has changed at this slinky bar/restaurant. Sax and trumpet solos still ring blissfully from the stage as jazz hounds sit back and sip martinis. *2060 rue Aylmer.* ☎ *514/842-8656. www. houseofjazz.ca. Cover C$3–C$8. Métro: McGill. Map p 102.*

The legendary Maison du Jazz is still the best place in town for jazz aficionados.

Singles favor the Sir Winston Churchill Pub Complex for after-work cocktails.

Newtown CENTRE-VILLE   Co-owned by one-hit Formula One racing wonder Jacques Villeneuve (Newtown's the English translation of his last name), this trendy multi-level nightspot is an oasis for the young, flirty, and sharply dressed. Sip cocktails in the ground-level bar or groove to the house music in the basement disco. *1476 rue Crescent.* ☎ *514/284-6555. www.newtown.ca. Métro: Peel. Map p 102.*

★ **Old Dublin Pub** CENTRE-VILLE   It's not much to look at, but this cozy and cheerful Irish pub is one of my favorites and only occasionally gets crowded. Other times, you can listen to the live music or to their U.K.-influenced playlist (such as the Scottish band Belle & Sebastian) while you sip a pint of Newcastle or an excellent single-malt scotch. *1219A rue University.* ☎ *514/ 861-4448. Métro: McGill. Map p 102.*

Peel Pub CENTRE-VILLE   This basement dive is (mystifyingly) one of the most popular bars among Americans looking to get drunk over the weekend, and there's almost always a line stretching up the stairs on Thursday and weekend nights. If you're with a large group, however, the oversized

and inexpensive beer can make it quite fun. *1107 rue Ste-Catherine ouest.* ☎ *514/844-7296. www. peelpub.com. Métro: Peel. Map p 102.*

★ **Roy Bar** PLATEAU   Back in my university days, this little hole-in-the-wall bar would get uncomfortably packed with college students avoiding the main crowd on St. Laurent. Not much has changed since then, with skateboarding videos still being played on the overhead TVs, kooky decorations randomly thrown on the walls, and cheap bottles of beer being downed by young, hipster-ish patrons. *351 rue Roy est.* ☎ *514/849-6467. Métro: Sherbrooke. Map p 101.*

Shed Café PLATEAU   This restaurant/bar is relatively unpretentious, especially in its rugged decor. At night, its great wine and scotch selection helps its local clientele relax and unwind; when day breaks, it becomes a trendy breakfast spot where the same partiers nurse their hangovers over eggs, bacon, and the morning paper. *3515 bd. St-Laurent.* ☎ *514/842-0220. Métro: Sherbrooke. Map p 101.*

Stogies CENTRE-VILLE   You'll almost always find a few businessmen puffing a Montecristo here after work. Later in the evening, a slightly older crowd gathers to sample the vast selection of cigars in the bar's humidor, or to sip one of the 101 martinis offered on the menu. *2015 rue Crescent.* ☎ *514/848-0069. www.stogiescigars.com. Métro: Peel. Map p 102.*

★ **Sir Winston Churchill Pub Complex** CENTRE-VILLE   One of rue Crescent's prime mingling spots, this landmark is where singles come to sip martinis or beer after a rough day at work. No matter when they stroll in, the young professionals that come to this three-floor meet market are always ready to flirt with new friends. *1459 rue Crescent.* ☎ *514/288-0623. www.swcpc.com. Métro: Guy-Concordia. Map p 102.*

Vinyl Lounge CENTRE-VILLE This dark cozy lounge's small setting is intimate, the music varied, and the clientele young. An assortment of DJs spin here on the weekends. *2109 rue de Bleury.* ☎ *514/844-7786. Métro: Place-des-Arts. Map p 102.*

Dance Clubs

Altitude 737 CENTRE-VILLE Locals dress up and saunter to the ground floor of Place Ville Marie, pass through the marble foyer and the bouncers, and hop into a special elevator that shoots guests straight to this top-level hot spot. Drinks can be pricey and the crowd is borderline prissy, but the view from the top of Montréal's tallest building, especially on pleasant nights when the terrace is open, makes this dance club unique. *1 place Ville Marie.* ☎ *514/296-4218. www.promoclub737.com. Cover C$8–C$12. Métro: Bonaventure. Map p 102.*

★ **Café Campus** PLATEAU Francophone Montréalers make up the majority of the dancers at the three-story Café Campus, but it's also popular with McGill students, who love the cheap drinks and good mix of '80s pop, contemporary hits, and (once in a while) Québécois tunes. On certain nights, indie acts or lesser-known musicians take to one of three stages. *57 rue Prince Arthur est.* ☎ *514/844-1010. www.cafecampus.com. Cover free–C$15. Map p 101.*

FunkyTown CENTRE-VILLE Play the part of John Travolta in *Saturday Night Fever* at this ritzy throwback to a forgettable decade where The BeeGees and Donna Summers still reign supreme. Who said disco is dead? *1454 rue Peel.* ☎ *514/282-8387. www.clubsmontreal.com. Cover C$5–C$10. Métro: Guy-Concordia. Map p 102.*

★★ **Jupiter Room** PLATEAU It usually takes quite a bit of coaxing to get me out on the dance floor, but 5 minutes in the very fun Jupiter Room got me out and gyrating without any pleading or dragging. There's something about the music (a mix of hits from every decade, cheesy and non-cheesy songs alike), laid-back crowd, and just the right amount of dim lighting that's conducive to unabashed arm-flailing. *3874 bd. St-Laurent.* ☎ *514/844-9696. Cover free to C$6. Métro: Sherbrooke or St-Laurent. Map p 101.*

Orchid PLATEAU This expansive and modern space has separate

The Old Dublin Pub serves a great selection of single-malt scotches.

Brutopia is the best bar in Montréal for beer lovers. See p 105.

lounging areas with plush couches, acres of dance floor drowning in hip-hop and R&B, and multiple bars where you can flirt and mingle with the extremely attractive clientele. Dress to the nines if you want to get in. *3556 bd. St-Laurent.* ☎ *514/848-6398. Cover up to C$15. Métro: Sherbrooke. Map p 101.*

★ **Stereo** QUARTIER LATIN   A landmark for hardcore partiers, this after-hours club is *the* destination of choice for the nocturnal, pumping out various forms of electronica from its impressive sound system. The party gets started at 2am and can go way past dawn. *858 rue Ste-Catherine est.* ☎ *514/286-0325. www.stereonightclub.com. Cover C$20–C$50. Métro: Berri-UQAM. Map p 101.*

★★★ **Tokyo Bar** PLATEAU   All dressed up and wish you could bust a move? This classy dance club—one of the best in Montréal—plays everything from hip-hop to disco for a mix of well-dressed regulars and tourists in their 20s and 30s. There's a rooftop terrace, a friendly and good-looking staff, a separate chill-out lounge, a dance floor, and a

room that sometimes features live music or a DJ. *3709 bd. St-Laurent.* ☎ *514/842-6838. www.tokyobar. com. Cover C$7–C$10. Métro: Sherbrooke or St-Laurent. Map p 101.*

Wine Bars

★★ **Modavie** VIEUX MONTREAL At night, one of Vieux Montréal's best restaurants puts its extensive wine selection to good use by becoming a busy wine and jazz bar. Musicians play jazz standards and bottles of aged scotch and rare wines are popped open for an entertaining and expensive evening. *1 rue St-Paul ouest.* ☎ *514/287-9582. Métro: Place d'Armes. Map p 102.*

Gay and Lesbian Bars and Clubs

★★ **Le Drugstore** CENTRE-VILLE Perhaps it's the bright, almost blinding, lights set throughout the place that draw gays, lesbians, and straights alike to this easygoing, ultra-popular gay club. Partiers will find boutiques, eateries, pool tables, a rooftop terrace, and a disco scattered among the eight floors. *1360 rue Ste-Catherine est.* ☎ *514/524-1960. Métro: Beaudry. Map p 104.*

★★ **Le Parking** QUARTIER LATIN This converted auto-repair shop is now one of the most fun gay bars in the city, thanks to a young crowd with a seemingly endless supply of energy. "Le Garage" in the basement provides more of a hip-hop and R&B vibe, while the top floor churns out bassy techno and electronica. Though it claims to be a mixed bar/club, Le Parking caters to a mostly male crowd looking for one-night stands.*1296 rue Amherst.* ☎ *514/522-2766. Cover varies. Métro: Beaudry. Map p 101.* ●

Arts & Entertainment Best Bets

Best **Free Live Music**
Pollack Concert Hall, *555 rue Sherbrooke ouest (p 117)*

Best **English-Speaking Theater**
★★★ Centaur Theatre, *453 rue St-Francois-Xavier (p 115)*

Best **Glitzy Repertory Theater**
★★ Ex-Centris, *3536 bd. St-Laurent (p 120)*

Best **Wacky Place to Watch a Play**
Infinitheatre, *5300 rue St-Dominique (p 115)*

Best **Theater for First-Run Films**
Paramount Theater, *977 rue Ste-Catherine (p 120)*

Best **Sports Venue**
★ Le Centre Bell, *1260 rue de la Gauchetiere ouest (p 120)*

Best **Stadium**
Molson Stadium, *Rue University (p 120)*

Best **Circus**
★★★ Cirque du Soleil *(p 116)*

Best **Refined Evening Entertainment**
★★ L'Orchestre Symphonique de Montréal (OSM) *(p 116)*

Most **Intimate Concert Venue**
★ Le Petit Campus, *57 rue Prince Arthur est (p 118)*

Best **Concert Venue for Big-Name Bands**
★ Le Centre Bell, *1260 rue de la Gauchetiere ouest (p 120)*

Best **Rock Concert Venue**
★★ Metropolis, *59 Ste-Catherine est (p 118)*

Best **Free Entertainment**
★ Theatre Verdure, *Parc Lafontaine (p 115)*

Best **Entertainment for Families**
Pepsi Forum, *rue Atwater and rue Ste-Catherine (p 119)*

Best **Comedy Spot**
★★ Comedy Nest, *2313 rue Ste-Catherine ouest (p 117)*

Best **Jazz Performances**
★★★ Maison de Jazz, *2060 rue Aylmer (p 107)*

Best **Jazz Restaurant**
★★ Modavie, *1 rue St-Paul ouest (p 110)*

Le Centre Bell is home to many of the city's concerts and its beloved Canadiens.

Previous page: Dame Edna in performance at the Theatre St-Denis.

A & E in **East Montréal**

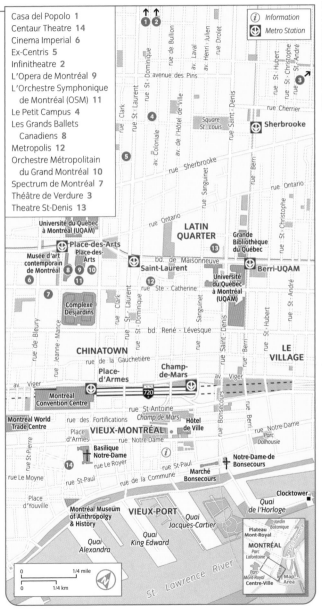

A & E in **West Montréal**

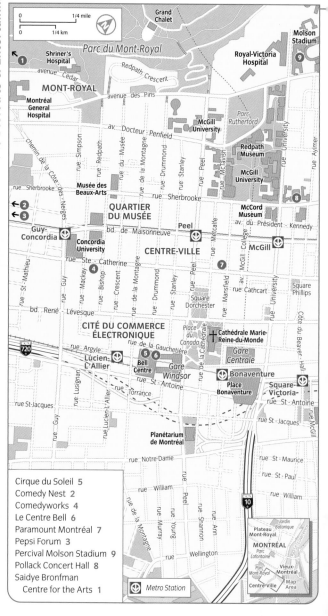

0   1/4 mile
0   1/4 km

Grand
Chalet

Molson
Stadium ❾

Parc du Mont-Royal

Shriner's
Hospital ❶

avenue Cedar

Royal-Victoria
Hospital

Redpath Crescent

MONT-ROYAL

Montréal
General
Hospital

avenue des Pins

Chemin de la Côte-des-Neiges

av. Docteur-Penfield

Parc
Rutherford

rue Simpson

rue Redpath

rue du Musée

rue de la Montagne

rue Drummond

rue Stanley

rue Peel

rue McTavish

McGill
University

Redpath
Museum

rue University

rue Aylmer

McGill
University

rue Sherbrooke

**Musée des
Beaux-Arts**

rue Sherbrooke

McCord
Museum ❽

**QUARTIER
DU MUSÉE**

av. du Président-Kennedy

Peel Ⓜ

❷ ←
❸ ←

bd. de Maisonneuve

rue Metcalfe

rue Peel

McGill-Collège

**Guy-
Concordia** Ⓜ

Concordia
University

CENTRE-VILLE

McGill Ⓜ

❼

rue Ste-Catherine

❹

rue Mackay

rue Bishop

rue Crescent

rue de la Montagne

rue Drummond

rue Stanley

rue Peel

rue Mansfield

av. Cathcart

rue University

Square
Phillips

rue St-Mathieu

rue Guy

bd. René-Lévesque

Square
Dorchester

Côte du Beaver-Hall

**CITÉ DU COMMERCE
ÉLECTRONIQUE**

rue de la Gauchetière

Place
du
Canada

✝ Cathédrale Marie-
Reine-du-Monde

720

rue Argyle

**Lucien-
L'Allier** Ⓜ

❺ ❻

**Bell
Centre**

rue de la Cathédrale

Gare
Centrale

rue Lusignan

rue St-Antoine

Gare
Windsor

Ⓜ **Bonaventure**

rue Guy

rue Lucien-L'Allier

rue Torrance

**Place
Bonaventure**

**Square-
Victoria-** Ⓜ

rue St-Antoine

rue St-Jacques

rue St-Jacques

rue McGill

**Planétarium
de Montréal**

rue Notre-Dame

rue St-Maurice

rue St-Paul

rue William

10

rue de la Montagne

rue Peel

rue Murray

rue Young

rue Shannon

rue Ann

rue Wellington

Ⓜ *Metro Station*

Jardin
Botanique

Plateau
Mont-Royal

MONTRÉAL

Parc
Lafontaine

Parc
Mont-Royal

Vieux-
Montréal

Centre-Ville

Map
Area

Montréal A & E A–Z

Theater

★★★ Centaur Theatre VIEUX MONTRÉAL This former stock exchange building (built in 1903) is now Montréal's primary English-speaking theater. Its reputation for showcasing some of the city's finest productions (from classics to modern Canadian drama) makes the theater a hot spot for tourists, and tickets to major plays here are usually hard to come by. *453 rue St-Francois-Xavier.* ☎ *514/288-3161. www.centaur theatre.com. Tickets from C$24. Métro: Place d'Armes. Map p 113.*

infinitheatre MILE END Installed in the formerly abandoned old Bain St-Michel, Montréal's quirkiest and most intriguing theater collaborates with some of the most talented theater companies in the country to provide Montréalers with the most cutting-edge and entertaining shows in Canada. *The Bain St-Michel, 5300 rue St-Dominique.* ☎ *514/987-1774, ext. 3. www.infinitheatre.com. Tickets from C$20, special events from C$75. Métro: Jean-Talon. Map p 113.*

★ Saidye Bronfman Centre for the Arts WESTMOUNT Named for noted philanthropist Saidye Bronfman (wife of Seagram founder Samuel Bronfman), the center is home to the Dora Wasserman Yiddish Theatre and the Leanor and Alvin Segal Theatre. Though many of the performances are staged in Yiddish, both theaters also present a number of English plays, such as *Amadeus* and *The Tempest.* *5170 Côte-Ste-Catherine (near bd. Décarie).* ☎ *514/739-7944. www. saidyebronfman.org. Tickets from C$15. Métro: Côte-Ste-Catherine. Bus: 29 Ouest. Map p 114.*

★ Théâtre de Verdure PLATEAU In summer, this outdoor theater in Parc Lafontaine is one of the best places in Montréal to enjoy a show or concert. Everything from L'Orchestre Symphonique de Montréal to free francophone and English films play this amazing venue, where admission is almost always free. *Parc Lafontaine.* ☎ *514/872-2644. Free admission. Métro: Sherbrooke. Map p 113.*

Theatre St-Denis QUARTIER LATIN Musicals, plays, and concerts in both English and French are performed in both of this historic theater's halls. Guffaws can be heard pouring out of the building when the Just for Laughs Festival uses the venue for its comedy events. *1594 rue St-Denis.* ☎ *514/790-1111. Tickets from C$25. Métro: Berri-UQAM.*

Theatrical performances are staged in both Yiddish and English at the Saidye Bronfman Centre for the Arts.

Circus

★★★ **Cirque du Soleil** A circus unlike any other, the internationally acclaimed Cirque du Soleil conjures up stunning performances that combine death-defying acrobatics, intense choreography, and incredibly vivid and colorful visuals set to engaging music. The troupe tours throughout the year, but if they happen to be in town, call the box office the first chance you get—the experience is worth every penny. *Office at 8400 2e av. St-Michel.* ☎ *800/361-4595 or 514/722-2324. www.cirquedusoleil.com. Ticket prices vary depending on venue. Map p 114.*

Dance

★ **Les Grands Ballets Canadiens** CENTRE VILLE When it isn't touring the globe, this internationally renowned ballet company performs almost exclusively in the Place des Arts. A breathtaking Christmas-season rendition of *The Nutcracker* is its most popular event of the year, but the critically acclaimed show *Romeo and Juliet* is also a classic. *Place des Arts, 175 Ste-Catherine ouest.* ☎ *514/842-2112. www.grand ballets.qc.ca. Tickets from C$25. Métro: Place des Arts. Map p 113.*

A production at the Centaur Theatre, Montréal's primary English theater. See p. 115.

The world-famous Cirque du Soleil is headquartered in Montréal, and many of its productions have premiered here.

Opera

★★ **L'Opera de Montréal** CENTRE VILLE Wonderful performances of timeless classics such as *Carmen* and *La Bohème* are clearly subtitled in French and English, though the video translations never interfere with the amazing sets below. Tickets can get pricey, but if you don't mind sacrificing perfection, heavily discounted tickets are sometimes available for final dress rehearsals that are nearly indistinguishable from the regular performances. *Salle Wilfrid-Pelletier, Place des Arts, 260 bd. de Maisonneuve ouest.* ☎ *514/985-2222. www.operade montreal.com. Tickets from C$40. Métro: Place des Arts. Map p 113.*

Classical Music & Concerts

★★ **L'Orchestre Symphonique de Montréal (OSM)** CENTRE VILLE One of the world's finest group of musicians plays a balanced lineup of classical works in several venues, including the Salle Wilfred-Pelletier of Place des Arts and Notre Dame Basilica. Students under age 25 can get heavily discounted tickets, subject to availability; other fans on a budget can attend one of the symphony's free summer concerts in Montréal's various parks. *Salle Wilfrid-Pelletier, Place des Arts, 260 bd. de Maisonneuve ouest.* ☎ *514/842-9951. www.osm.ca. Tickets from C$20. Métro: Place des Arts. Map p 113.*

Orchestre Métropolitain du Grand Montréal CENTRE VILLE Performing classics by composers such as Debussy, Stravinsky, and Mozart in various venues, the talented Metropolitan Orchestra also often collaborates with other groups, especially L'Opera de Montréal. It occasionally even outshines its more celebrated rival, L'Orchestre Symphonique de Montréal. *Maisonneuve Theatre, Place des Arts, 260 bd. de Maisonneuve ouest.* ☎ *514/598-0870. Tickets from C$20. Métro: Place des Arts. Map p 113.*

Pollack Concert Hall CENTRE VILLE A stone statue of Queen Victoria perched on her throne guards the entrance to this landmark (1908) building on the McGill University campus, where many classical concerts and recitals are staged. Because most of the concerts are by McGill students or alumni, tickets are more affordable (most are free) than those for performances in Place des Arts. *555 rue Sherbrooke ouest.* ☎ *514/398-4547. www.music.mcgill.ca. Tickets free– C$30. Métro: McGill. Map p 114.*

The Theatre St-Denis fills with laughter during the Just for Laughs comedy festival. See p. 115.

Comedy

★★ **Comedy Nest** CENTRE VILLE When Ernie Butler, one of the city's funniest radio personalities, isn't making people laugh on the AM dial, he's running Montréal's best comedy club, The Comedy Nest. You'll usually find hilarious sketches or gut-bustingly funny improv acts on any given night, and during the Juste pour Rire Festival, the club serves as one of the performance areas for comedians. *In the Pepsi Forum, 2313 rue Ste-Catherine ouest.* ☎ *514/932-6378. www.the comedynest.com. Tickets to regular performances C$12 adults, C$6 students. Métro: Atwater. Map p 114.*

★ **Comedyworks** CENTRE VILLE Comedyworks entertains patrons every day with improvisational groups and open-mic nights. As

The Orchestre Métropolitain du Grand Montréal performs in venues around the city.

The post-modern Ex-Centris is best for those who like French films. See p. 120.

funny as the improv groups are, the best time to come is on weekends, when well-known comedians (Jon Stewart's made an appearance) take to the stage. *1238 rue Bishop.* ☎ *514/398-9661. www.fluidicweb. com/webcom. Cover from C$5. Métro: Guy-Concordia. Map p 114.*

Jazz & Rock Concert Venues
★★ **Casa del Popolo** MILE END In addition to drawing local musicians and low-key indie acts such as Damien Jurado and Rosie Thomas, the cozy Casa del Popolo also holds a yearly music festival during the summer. The performance space is tiny (more or less just a cleared-out corner in the back), but all musical genres are well represented and it's a surprisingly popular place. *4873 bd. St-Laurent.* ☎ *514/284-3804. www.casadelpopolo.com. Tickets C$5–C$15, cover C$5–C$10. Métro: Laurier. Map p 113.*

★ **Le Petit Campus** CENTRE VILLE This small and intimate venue (room for no more than 50 people) is sheltered from the bassy beats of the adjacent Café Campus, and often features lesser-known indie bands or fledgling local artists. Bands and musicians, such as Clem Snide, are underrated enough that you'll usually be able to get tickets at the door.

57 rue Prince Arthur est. ☎ *514/844-1010. www.cafecampus.com. Tickets for concerts C$8–C$20. Métro: Sherbrooke. Map p 113.*

★★ **Metropolis** CENTRE VILLE Established bands and big-name musicians that haven't quite reached stadium/arena status are the headliners at this prime downtown venue. It usually sees its main floor fill up to its 2,000-person capacity thanks to the likes of performers such as Blondie, The Roots, and local legend Jean Leloup. *59 Ste-Catherine est.* ☎ *514/844-3500. www.spectrumdemontreal.ca/metro polis. Tickets C$10–C$30. Map p 113. Métro: St-Laurent.*

★★ **Spectrum de Montréal** CENTRE VILLE   Bands play the Spectrum for two reasons: They're almost ready to play in the larger Metropolis, or the Metropolis is already booked up. Either way, the more centrally located Spectrum hosts musicians from the city's red-hot indie scene as well as forgettable Québécois and American groups. *318 rue Ste-Catherine ouest.* ☎ *800/361-4595 or 514/861-5851. www.spectrumdemontreal.ca/ spectrum. Tickets from C$12. Métro: Place des Arts. Map p 113.*

Entertainment Venues
★ **Le Centre Bell** CENTRE VILLE This dazzling facility, Montréal's largest all-purpose entertainment venue, allows for all sorts of different stage arrangements and sports configurations. As a result, it's home to hockey's Montréal Canadiens (p 155), but also plays host to such renowned rock and pop groups as U2 and Aerosmith, and to cultural acts such as Cirque du Soleil. *1260 rue de la Gauchetiere ouest.* ☎ *514/790-1245 or 514/989-2841 for box office. www.centrebell.ca. Métro: Lucien L'Allier or Bonaventure. Map p 114.*

A Night with Lady Luck

Québec's first casino, **Casino de Montréal** (☎ 800/665-2274 or 514/392-2746; www.casino-de-Montréal.com), is in the former French Pavilion, left over from the 1967 Expo World's Fair, on Île Notre-Dame. The adjacent Québec Pavilion was incorporated into the complex in 1996. The multilevel casino is open round the clock and contains more than 120 game tables, including roulette, craps, blackjack, and baccarat; and more than 3,200 slot machines. It's also home to a selection of good restaurants, four bars, and live theatrical shows, that usually pay tribute to legendary stars (Sinatra, Streisand, and Ray Charles, just to name a few). Tickets to the cabaret can be purchased at the casino or on the Internet at **www.admission.com**.

Patrons must be 18 or over. The originally strict dress code has been relaxed somewhat, but the following items of clothing are still prohibited: "cut-off sweaters and shirts, tank tops, jogging outfits, cut-off shorts and bike shorts, beachwear, work or motorcycle boots, and clothing associated with violence or with an organization known to be violent." To get to the casino, take the Métro to the Île Ste-Hélène stop, which is adjacent to Île Notre-Dame, and walk or take the shuttle bus from there. There's also an hourly shuttle bus *(navette)* from the Infotouriste Centre at 1001 rue du Square-Dorchester.

Pepsi Forum CENTRE VILLE The former home of the NHL's Montréal Canadiens (the seats on the main floor are the originals) was transformed into this sprawling multistory entertainment complex. It's home to a 22-screen multiplex, a restaurant and bar, a dance club, the Comedy Nest (p 117), and separate areas where you can play video games, bowl a few frames, and hustle your pals at pool. *Rue Atwater and Rue Ste-Catherine. Métro: Atwater. Prices vary by venue. Map p 114.*

Film
★★ **Cinema Imperial** CENTRE VILLE After years of renovation, this fixture of the World Film Festival (it opened in 1905) has finally reopened its doors to the public, though screenings are currently limited to special events and movie openings. The sleek, modern exterior hides a majestic single-screen theater and a regal balcony that has been wonderfully refurbished. *1432 rue de Bleury. Call for showtimes and ticket prices:* ☎ *514/848-7187. Métro: Place des Arts. Map p 113.*

The Casino de Montréal.

★★ **Ex-Centris** PLATEAU   Many of the films shown on the three state-of-the-art screens at the swank post-modern Ex-Centris are shown only in French. But if you're bilingual or happen to be in town when they have an English release, dinner and a movie on glitzy St-Laurent can be an interesting (albeit expensive) event. *3536 bd. St-Laurent.* ☎ *514/847-2206. www.ex-centris.com. Tickets C$10 adults (C$7.50 Mon and matinees), C$7 students and seniors, C$6 kids under 12. Métro: St-Laurent. Map p 113.*

Paramount Montréal CENTRE VILLE   The construction of Montréal's most profitable multiplex in the late '90s all but sealed the fates of smaller, cheaper theaters on rue Ste-Catherine. The behemoth shows the latest blockbusters on 13 screens, including a six-story IMAX version with gargantuan speakers totaling hundreds of watts. *977 rue Ste-Catherine.* ☎ *514/842-5828. www.cineplex.com. Tickets from C$11. Métro: Peel. Map p 114.*

Spectator Sports
★ **Le Centre Bell** CENTRE VILLE The former Molson Centre has been home to the city's beloved Montréal Canadiens since 1996. Join the loyal Habs fans populating the red cheap seats in the upper deck (called the

The modern Paramount Montréal is the city's most popular multiplex.

The former home of the Montréal Canadiens, the Pepsi Forum is now an all-purpose entertainment center, but has hung on to reminders of its hockey past. See p. 119.

Molson-Ex Zone) of this massive arena as they cheer on their (recently luckless) hockey heroes. *1260 rue de la Gauchetiere ouest.* ☎ *514/790-1245 for tickets. www.canadiens.com. Tickets C$16–C$100. Métro: Lucien L'Allier or Bonaventure. Map p 114.*

Percival Molson Stadium CENTRE VILLE   During the Canadian Football League (CFL) season, this stadium gets incredibly loud on Sundays thanks to the die-hard, chest-painting Montréal Alouettes (that's French for "larks") fans that blow incessantly into their deafening plastic horns to create quite a ruckus. Thanks to the team's recent playoff success (and a Stanley Cup drought coupled with the departure of the city's baseball team a few year's back) the Alouettes' reputation has skyrocketed with locals. Needless to say, tickets to games at this venerable stadium (it was built in 1916 and named for a sporting McGill alumni) sell out quickly. *Top of rue University (McGill University campus).* ☎ *514/871-2255 for Alouettes tickets and info. www.alouettes.net. Tickets C$21–C$82. Métro: McGill. Map p 114.* ●

Hotel Best Bets

Best **Business Hotel**
★★ Fairmont The Queen Elizabeth, $$$–$$$$ *900 bd. René-Lévesque ouest (p 126)* and Hôtel Gault, $$$–$$$$$ *449 rue Ste-Hélène (p 127)*

Best **Historic Hotel**
The Ritz-Carlton Montréal, $$–$$$$ *1228 rue Sherbrooke ouest (p 130)* and Hôtel Le St-James, $$$$$ *355 rue St-Jacques (p 128)*

Best **Hip Hotel**
★★★ W Montréal, $$$$$ *901 rue Square Victoria (p 130)*

Best **Bed & Breakfast**
★★ Auberge du Vieux-Port, $$$ *97 rue de la Commune est (p 125)*

Best **Lodging in Vieux-Montréal**
Hôtel Le St-James, $$$$$ *355 rue St-Jacques (p 128)*

Best **Moderately Priced Hotel**
★ Le Meridien Versailles, $$$ *1808 rue Sherbrooke ouest (p 129)*

Best **for Families**
★ Delta Montréal, $$ *475 av. du President-Kennedy (p 126)*

Best **Location**
★★ Fairmont The Queen Elizabeth, $$$–$$$$ *900 bd. René-Lévesque ouest (p 126)*

Best **Cheap Bed**
McGill Residences (RVC), $ *3425 rue University (p 130)*

Best **for Romance**
★★ Auberge du Vieux-Port, $$$ *97 rue de la Commune est (p 125)*

Best **Value**
Auberge Les Passants San Soucy, $$ *171 rue St-Paul ouest (p 125)*

Previous Page: Bedroom in the Hotel Place D'Armes.

The antiques-filled Hôtel Le St-James is Montréal's best choice for traditional but luxurious accommodations.

Best **Modern Hotel**
★★★ W Montréal, $$$$$ *901 rue Square Victoria (p 130)*

Best **Hotel Staff**
Château Versailles, $$$ *1659 rue Sherbrooke ouest (p 125)*

Best **Downtown Hotel**
★★★ Sofitel, $$$–$$$$ *1155 rue Sherbrooke ouest (p 130)*

Best **Views**
★★ Auberge du Vieux-Port, $$$ *97 rue de la Commune est (p 125)*

Best **for Backpackers**
Auberge de Jeunesse, $ *1030 rue Mackay (p 125)*

Best **Health Club**
★★ Hôtel Omni Mont-Royal, $$–$$$ *1050 rue Sherbrooke ouest (p 128)*

Best **Bathrooms**
★★ Loews Hôtel Vogue, $$–$$$$ *1425 rue de la Montagne (p 129)*

Best **Boutique Hotel**
★★★ Hôtel Le Germain, $$$ *2050 rue Mansfield (p 128)*

123

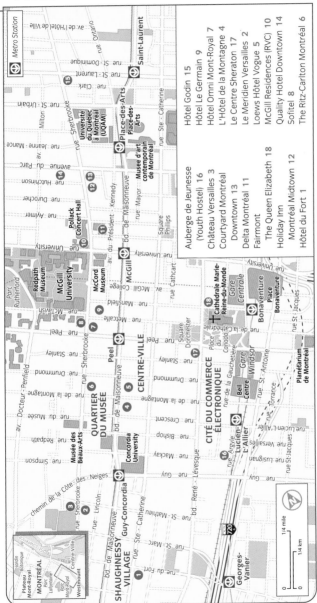

Auberge de Jeunesse (Youth Hostel) 16
Château Versailles 3
Courtyard Montréal Downtown 13
Delta Montréal 14
Fairmont The Queen Elizabeth 18
Holiday Inn Montréal Midtown 12
Hôtel du Fort 1

Hôtel Godin 15
Hôtel Le Germain 9
Hôtel Omni Mont-Royal 7
L'Hôtel de la Montagne 4
Le Centre Sheraton 17
Le Meridien Versailles 2
Loews Hôtel Vogue 5
McGill Residences (RVC) 10
Quality Hotel Downtown 14
Sofitel 8
The Ritz-Carlton Montréal 6

Vieux-Montréal Hotels

Auberge Bonaparte 9
Auberge Les Passants
du Sans Soucy 10
Auberge du Place Royal 12
Auberge du Vieux-Port 13
Hostellerie Pierre du Calvet 14
Hôtel Gault 4
Hôtel Inter-Continental Montréal 2

Hôtel Le St-James 6
Hôtel Le Saint-Sulpice 7
Hôtel Nelligan 11
Hôtel St-Paul 8
Hôtel XIXe Siècle 5
Le Place d'Armes
Hôtel & Suites 3
W Montréal 1

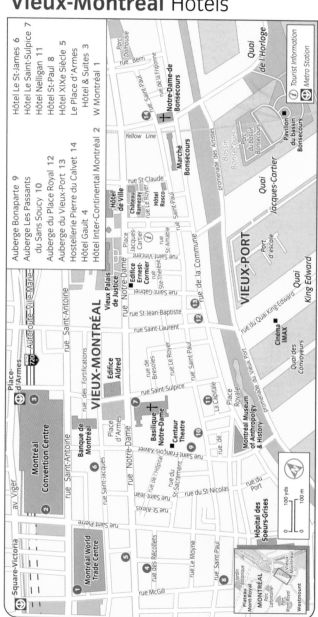

Hotels A to Z

★ **Auberge Bonaparte** VIEUX-MONTREAL Housed in a charming 1886 building, this romantic inn's furnishings may be humble, but the smoke-free rooms are tastefully decorated and the cozy terrace on the roof provides beautiful views of the Vieux Montréal. *447 rue St-François-Xavier.* ☎ *514/844-1448. www. bonaparte.com. 31 units. Doubles C$145–C$355. AE, DC, MC, V. Métro: Place d'Armes or Square Victoria. Map p 124.*

Auberge de Jeunesse (Youth Hostel) CENTRE-VILLE One of the best hostels in the city is a bit of a hike to St-Laurent, and the metal bunk beds can be a little creaky, but with rue Crescent's bars and clubs a few minutes away you probably won't want to sleep anyway. *1030 rue Mackay.* ☎ *514/843-3317. www.hostellingMontreal.com. About 240 beds. Single bed C$30, private rooms C$75. AE, MC, V. Map p 123.*

Auberge Les Passants du Sans Soucy VIEUX-MONTREAL One of the first places travelers should look for accommodations if they want to stay in Vieux-Montréal. Rooms captivate guests with such rustic touches as exposed brick, wood-beamed ceilings, and small fireplaces. *171 rue St-Paul ouest.*

☎ *514/842-2634. www.lesanssoucy. com. 9 units. Doubles C$115–C$185. AE, DC, MC, V. Métro: Place d'Armes. Map p 124.*

Auberge du Place Royal VIEUX-MONTREAL If you're willing to sacrifice a few bells and whistles, book a room at this inn, which isn't as plush as some similarly romantic spots but is a fraction of their price. Most rooms offer an unobstructed view of the waterfront. *115 rue de la Commune Ouest.* ☎ *514/287-0522. www.aubergeplaceroyale.com/en. 12 units. Doubles C$135–C$195. AE, MC, V. Map p 124.*

★★ **Auberge du Vieux-Port** VIEUX-MONTREAL Honeymooners and lovebirds on weekend getaways adore the cozy and smoke-free rooms at this 1882-built luxury inn. In addition to modern creature comforts, you'll find rustic stone walls and wooden beams, as well as picture-perfect views of the waterfront. *97 rue de la Commune est.* ☎ *888/ 660-7678 or 514/876-0081. www. aubergeduvieuxport.com. 27 units. Doubles C$175–C$380. AE, DC, DISC, MC, V. Métro: Champ-de-Mars. Map p 124.*

★ **Château Versailles** CENTRE-VILLE This boutique hotel's extremely professional and amiable

A bedroom at the Auberge Les Passants du Sans Soucy, a quintessential Old Montréal hotel.

A deluxe room at the atmospheric Château Versailles.

staff bends over backwards to ensure a pleasant stay (and will lug your baggage up the stairs of the quaint but elevator-free pre–World War I building). *1659 rue Sherbrooke ouest.* ☎ *888/933-8111 or 514/933-8111. www.versailleshotels.com. 65 units. Doubles C$255–C$295. AE, DC, MC, V. Métro: Guy. Map p 123.*

kids Courtyard Montréal Downtown CENTRE-VILLE With coin-operated washing machines, an indoor pool, a major grocery store half a block away, and reasonable prices, the Courtyard is perfect for families on an extended stay in Montréal. Its location on Sherbrooke is also a great starting point for sightseers. *410 rue Sherbrooke ouest.* ☎ *800/449-6654 or 514/844-8855. www.courtyard.com. 181 units. Doubles C$159–C$399. AE, DC, MC, V. Métro: Place des Arts. Map p 123.*

★ **kids Delta Montréal** CENTRE-VILLE Primarily a business hotel (with all of the amenities that implies), the Delta is also superb for families thanks to two pools, a supervised play center, huge guest rooms, and a reasonably priced spa. *475 av. du President-Kennedy.* ☎ *877/286-1986 or 514/286-1986. www.delta Montréal.com. 453 units. Doubles C$159–C$450. AE, DC, MC, V. Métro: McGill. Map p 123.*

★★ **Fairmont The Queen Elizabeth** CENTRE-VILLE The city's largest and most convenient hotel—where John and Yoko staged their famous 1969 "bed-in"—sits atop Gare Centrale. The "Queenie" goes to great lengths when it comes to guests' comfort and is much beloved by the executives who make up its primary clientele. *900 bd. René-Lévesque ouest.* ☎ *800/441-1414 or 514/861-3511. www.fairmont.com. 1,039 units. Doubles C$209–C$450. AE, DC, MC, V. Métro: Bonaventure. Map p 123.*

Holiday Inn Montréal Midtown CENTRE-VILLE This no-frills member of the popular chain has all the expected amenities, and is a good option for a last-minute vacancy when everything else in town is booked up. The hotel's great location more than makes up for the standard semi-soft beds, the stiff sheets, and the even stiffer personality of the front desk staff. *420 rue Sherbrooke ouest.* ☎ *800/288-4595 or 514/842-2611. www.holidayinn.com. 487 units. Doubles C$100–C$135. AE, DC, MC, V. Métro: Place des Arts. Map p 123.*

★★ **Hostellerie Pierre du Calvet** VIEUX-MONTREAL For the ultimate old-world experience (you get air-conditioning, but no TVs), book one of the luxurious rooms in this museum-like inn, which was built in 1725. Most of the furniture and decor, from the carpets to the sofas to the artwork, are original antiques that date as far back as the

A bedroom at the historic Fairmont The Queen Elizabeth.

The indoor pool at the Delta Montréal is just one the amenities that makes this hotel great for families.

18th century. *405 rue Bonsecours.*
☎ *866/544-1725 or 514/282-1725.*
www.pierreducalvet.ca. 10 units.
Doubles C$265–C$295. AE, MC, V.
Métro: Place d'Armes or Champ-de-Mars. Map p 124.

Hôtel du Fort CENTRE-VILLE   A
favorite of business travelers, this
reliable hotel on the edges of downtown has good-sized bedrooms with
separate sitting areas and basic
kitchenettes that include fridges and
microwave ovens. Skip the mediocre
buffet breakfast if it isn't included in
your rate and eat at one of the many
nearby cafes. *1390 rue du Fort.*
☎ *800/565-6333 or 514/939-8333.*
www.hoteldufort.com. 124 units.
Doubles C$135–C$175. AE, DC, MC, V.
Métro: Atwater.

★★ Hôtel Gault VIEUX-MONTREAL
This small boutique hotel—one of
Montréal's finest—is home to 30
uniquely designed rooms, running
the gamut from minimalist chic to
old-world romantic to business prac-
tical. The living spaces do have one
commonality: unparalleled comfort.
449 rue Ste-Hélène. ☎ *866/904-1616
or 514/904-1616. www.hotelgault.
com. 30 units. Doubles C$229–C$749.
AE, DC, MC, V. Métro: Square Victoria. Map p 124.*

★★ Hôtel Godin CENTRE-VILLE
An ultramodern luxury inn for the
rich and hip—and, unusual for the
city, their pets. The minimalist but

roomy accommodations offer high-
tech toys, such as LCD TVs, and very
comfy bedding. *10 rue Sherbrooke
ouest.* ☎ *866/744-6346 or 514/843-
6000. www.hotelgodin.com. 136
units. Doubles C$250–C$425. AE, DC,
MC, V. Métro: St-Laurent. Map p 123.*

**★★ Hôtel Inter-Continental
Montréal** VIEUX-MONTREAL   It's
not luxurious by any means, but the
city's premier choice for business
travelers does have some hints of
quaint character, including its historic
1888 Nordheimer Building and glass-
enclosed courtyard (formerly Fortifi-
cation Lane). Guest rooms are quite
comfortable, however, with king-size
beds and plenty of workspace for
execs. *360 rue St-Antoine ouest.*
☎ *800/361-3600 or 514/987-9900.
www.Montreal.intercontinental.com.
357 units. Doubles C$145–C$440.
AE, DC, DISC, MC, V. Métro: Square
Victoria. Map p 124.*

*The sophisticated Hôtel Le Germain is a
bastion of modern comfort. See p. 128.*

★★★ **Hôtel Le Germain** CENTRE-VILLE   You won't want to leave the coddling grasp of this sublime boutique hotel, thanks to its wonderful staff, visually engaging rooms, incredible beds, delicious breakfast, and fantastic amenities. The level of sophistication means families may want to stay elsewhere. *2050 rue Mansfield.* ☎ *877/ 333-2050 or 514/849-2050. www. hotelboutique.com. 101 units. Doubles C$210–C$275. AE, DC, MC, V. Métro: Peel. Map p 123.*

★★★ **Hôtel Le St-James** VIEUX-MONTRÉAL   The top choice in Montréal for affluent travelers looking to eschew ultramodern style without sacrificing luxury. Each antiques-laden room in this 1870 building could easily double as an Old Montréal landmark, but all sport a full range of amenities. *355 rue St-Jacques.* ☎ *866/841-3111 or 514/841-3111. www.hotellestjames.com. 61 units. Doubles C$400–C$495. AE, DC, MC, V. Métro: Square Victoria. Map p 124.*

★★ kids **Hôtel Le Saint-Sulpice** VIEUX-MONTRÉAL   This elite all-suite hotel is a great choice for the families who can afford its high price tag. Among the numerous in-room perks are a mini-kitchen, separate seating areas, multiple TVs, and fireplaces and/or balconies in many

The marble bathrooms at Le Place d'Armes Hotel & Suites, have such first-rate amenities as flatscreen TVs and separate showers. See p 129.

The all-suite Hôtel Le Saint-Sulpice is a great option for families looking for extra room.

of the suites. *414 rue St-Sulpice.* ☎ *877/785-7423 or 514/288-1000. www.lesaintsulpice.com. 108 units. Doubles C$189–C$569. AE, DC, MC, V. Métro: Place d'Armes. Map p 124.*

★★★ **Hôtel Nelligan** VIEUX-MONTRÉAL   Named for a famous Québec poet—quotes from his works are plastered on the guest room walls—this fashionable hotel impresses with such pluses as down duvets on the cozy beds, and CD players that help lull guests to sleep. Night owls will appreciate the lounge that hums with activity late into the evening. *106 rue St-Paul ouest.* ☎ *877/788-2040 or 514/788-2040. www.hotelnelligan.com. 63 units. Doubles C$190–C$465. AE, DC, MC, V. Métro: Square Victoria. Map p 124.*

★★ **Hôtel Omni Mont-Royal** CENTRE-VILLE   The exterior of the Omni is largely overlooked by passersby, but inside, this luxury hotel shines. Standard upper-crust offerings of robes and CD players in the rooms, as well as the city's best health club and spa, help guests (a mix of execs, honeymooners, and the well-to-do) relax and unwind in comfort. *1050 rue Sherbrooke ouest.* ☎ *514/284-1110. www.omnihotels.com. 299 units. Doubles C$139–C$299. AE, DC, MC, V. Métro: Peel. Map p 123.*

★★ **Hôtel St-Paul** VIEUX-MONTRÉAL   A chic and upscale alternative to some of Old Montréal's more dignified establishments. The bright but comfortable rooms and their frenzied furnishings sport all the modern conveniences and are a stark contrast to the hotel's dark hallways. *355 rue McGill.* ☎ *866/380-2202 or 514/380-2222. www.hotelstpaul.com. 120 units. Doubles C$205–C$500. AE, DC, MC, V. Métro: Square Victoria. Map p 124.*

Hôtel XIXe Siècle VIEUX-MONTREAL The Second Empire interiors of this quiet boutique hotel reflect its 1870 origins as the Montréal City and District Savings Bank, with incredibly high ceilings and a Victorian-style lobby. One of the bank's vaults has been converted to a small bedroom; the other guest rooms are spacious, and many have whirlpool tubs. *262 rue St-Jacques.* ☎ *877/553-0019 or 514/985-0019. www.hotelxixsiecle.com. 59 units. Doubles C$140–C$395. AE, DC, MC, V. Métro: Square Victoria.*

★ **L'Hôtel de la Montagne** CENTRE-VILLE A grand impression left by the lobby's gilded fairy and her stained-glass wings fades once guests enter the standard rooms, whose furnishings seem more outmoded than antique. Even so, it's an extremely comfortable place to stay. *1430 rue de la Montagne.* ☎ *800/361-6262 or 514/288-5656. www.hoteldelamontagne.com. 136 units. Doubles C$185–C$225. AE, MC, V. Métro: Peel. Map p 123.*

★ **Le Centre Sheraton** CENTRE-VILLE This modern business hotel caters primarily to the suit-and-tie crowd. The central location, good-size rooms, and numerous amenities (including a pool) make it a good choice for leisure travelers,

The friendly staff and comfortable rooms at Le Meridien Versailles make it a good bet.

The dining room at the top notch Loews Hôtel Vogue.

too. *1201 bd. René-Lévesque ouest.* ☎ *514/878-2000. www.sheraton.com/lecentre. 825 units. Doubles C$179–C$590. AE, DC, DISC, MC, V. Métro: Bonaventure or Peel. Map p 123.*

★ **Le Meridien Versailles** CENTRE-VILLE Among the best of the Montréal hotels that haven't quite reached luxury status, modern Le Meridien lures a variety of travelers with large, comfortably furnished rooms and superlative service by a very friendly staff (who once checked me in without an ounce of ID after I lost my wallet on the way there—and then facilitated a meeting with the kind soul who found it). *1808 rue Sherbrooke ouest.* ☎ *888/933-8111 or 514/933-8111. www.versailleshotels.com. 106 units. Doubles C$269–C$279. AE, DC, MC, V. Métro: Guy. Map p 123.*

★★ **Le Place d'Armes Hôtel & Suites** VIEUX-MONTREAL Not quite as exquisite as the late 19th-century architecture of the building housing them, the amenity-laden guest rooms are still reasonably plush. One of the prime places to stay in Montréal. *55 rue St-Jacques ouest.* ☎ *888/450-1887 or 514/842-1887. www.hotelplacedarmes.com. 48 units. Doubles C$185–C$290. AE, DC, DISC, MC, V. Métro: Place d'Armes. Map p 124.*

★★ **Loews Hôtel Vogue** CEN-TRE-VILLE This top-notch hotel is no longer hip, but provides enough luxury and comfort to draw high-profile guests. The decadent marble bathrooms—with Jacuzzis, separate showers, flatscreen TVs, and lighted

The Best Hotels

The stylish Sofitel caters to celebrities with first-class rooms and amenities.

make-up mirrors—are the best in town. *1425 rue de la Montagne. ☎ 800/465-6654 or 514/285-5555. www.loewshotels.com. 142 units. Doubles C$159–C$399. AE, DC, DISC, MC, V. Métro: Peel. Map p 123.*

McGill Residences (RVC) CENTRE-VILLE   During the summer semesters, McGill University opens their residence halls to visitors, who can rent (mostly single) rooms with shared bathrooms. The best of the bunch are the dorms at the centrally located Royal Victoria College. *3425 rue University. ☎ 514/398-5200. www. mcgill.ca/residences/summer. Doubles C$49 (most rooms are singles). MC, V. Métro: McGill. Map p 123.*

Quality Hotel Downtown CEN-TRE-VILLE   It's usually filled with thrifty travelers, as well as casual vacationers from New York and Vermont. Take advantage of the moderately priced budget-style accommodations, but skip the breakfast (extra charge) in favor of the more attractive Chez Cora (p 123) option across the street. *3440 av. du Parc. ☎ 514/849-1413. www.choicehotels.com. 140 units. Doubles C$120–C$165. AE, DC, MC, V. Métro: Place des Arts. Map p 123.*

★★ The Ritz-Carlton Montréal CENTRE-VILLE   One of the city's most prestigious hotels, the Ritz-Carlton boasts large, traditionally styled rooms; excellent bathrooms, a very

high level of service, and prices that aren't as stratospheric as some of the other luxury properties in town. Prepare to be treated like royalty at this landmark, which has been attracting the rich and famous for nearly a century. *1228 rue Sherbrooke ouest. ☎ 800/363-0366 or 514/842-4212. www.ritzcarlton.com/ hotels/Montreal. 230 units. Doubles C$160–C$325. AE, DC, MC, V. Métro: Peel. Map p 123.*

★★★ Sofitel CENTRE-VILLE   Executives and celebrities alike are drawn to this modern hotel for its top-notch hospitality and exclusivity. Rooms are filled with the latest in creature comforts, from goose-down comforters to CD players, and the excellent health club is open round-the-clock. *1155 rue Sherbrooke ouest. ☎ 877/285-9001 or 514/285-9000. www.sofitel.com. 258 units. Doubles C$190–C$675. AE, DC, DISC, MC, V. Métro: Peel. Map p 123.*

★★★ W Montréal VIEUX-MONTREAL   For the young, hip, and attractive (definitely not for families or conservative travelers), the brazen W serves up a cool party-time atmosphere that includes plush, high-tech bedrooms equipped with bathrooms that offer little privacy, and a raucous bar that stays open until the wee hours of the morning. *901 rue Square Victoria. ☎ 888/625-5144 or 514/395-3100. www.whotels.com/ Montréal. 152 units. Doubles C$349–C$819. AE, DC, MC, V. Métro: Square Victoria. Map p 124.* ●

The high-tech rooms at the W Montréal are some of the pushest in town.

The Laurentians

Where to Stay

1. Val David
2. Parc Aquatique du Mont St-Sauveur
3. Mont Tremblant
4. Lac Tremblant
5. Circuit Mont Tremblant

Where to Stay

6. Auberge Edelweiss
7. Fairmont Mont Tremblant
8. Quintessence
9. Youth Hostel Tremblant

Where to Dine

10. Antipasto
11. Aux Truffes

Previous Page: Skiers riding to the top of Mont-Tremblant.

Among the oldest in the world, the modest mountain ranges of the Laurentians (aka the Laurentides), set 55 to 129km (34–80 miles) north of Montréal, provide year-round recreational opportunities for those seeking escape from the hustle and bustle of the city. Skiing and snowboarding are most popular activities, but the best way to enjoy the Laurentians is to explore the scenic region's trails in the warmer months, when the mountain has thawed and reveals the beautiful natural surroundings. Enjoy the views as you travel through the area's verdant forests or sail its exquisite lakes. Note that the region is best explored over the course of a 2- to 3-day side trip. START: **To take advantage of this tour, you'll need to rent a car. Head north out of Montréal on Autoroute 15. Take exit 76 to Val David.**

1 Val David. The sleepy town of Val David often gets overlooked by tourists whizzing by on their way to Mont-Tremblant. Their loss is your gain because here are acres of breathtaking trails for mountain bikers and hikers (as well as snowshoers and cross-country skiers in the winter) waiting for those who know of their existence. The North River and the surrounding rock faces also provide the perfect conditions for kayakers (try **Pause Plein Air,** 1381 chemin de la Sapiniére; ☎ 877/422-6880 or 819/322-6880; C\$30 for daylong kayak rental, C\$60

A home in sleepy Val David, a mecca for skiers in winter and hikers in summer.

for daylong canoe rental) and rock climbers. Residents go so far as to boast that Val David is the birthplace of rock climbing in Eastern Canada. And unlike the heavily visited Mont-Tremblant, where cheesy souvenir stores are plentiful, Val David is home to a handful of fantastic little stores that sell well-made, authentic crafts, particularly ceramics. If you find yourself in Val David in the middle of the summer season, make sure to check out its enormous ceramic art festival, 1001Pots (www.1001pots.com), which runs from mid-July to mid-August. *Tourist office at 2501 rue de l'Église.* ☎ 888/322-7030. www.valdavid.com.

Spend the night in Val David before driving 50km (31 miles) along Route 117 to Mont-Tremblant (making a right at the Rte. 327 turnoff at St-Jovite) the next morning. Check into your hotel and then make your way south on Route 117 to Mont St-Sauveur (69km/43 miles from Mont-Tremblant).

2 ★ kids Parc Aquatique du Mont St-Sauveur. The flumes and slides at Canada's biggest water park help visitors and locals forget the stifling and humid summer heat they left behind in Montréal. The region's summer tourist hot spot

Part of the charm of visiting the Laurentians is driving through the region's picturesque towns.

can get crowded on weekends in July and August, but you'll never feel claustrophobic thanks to the park's smart layout. Once you see the hordes of giddy and soaked vacationers running from ride to ride, you'll understand why Montréalers make the drive up to the Laurentians in the middle of the summer. The Colorado River is the most popular attraction, but adventurous visitors should try the Grand Remous River ride, a 20-minute journey down a set of rapids. *350 rue St- Denis. ☎ 800/363-2426 or 450/227-4671. www.parcaquatique.com. Open early June through early September. Tickets C$14–C$30.*

Spend an afternoon (2–3 hr.) splashing around the park before retreating to your hotel in Mont-Tremblant. Travel north on Route 117 and head right at the Route 327 turnoff to get back to the mountain.

❸ ★★★ **Mont-Tremblant.** The Laurentian's tallest peak stands at a height of 650m (2,132 ft.) and was named after an Amerindan legend that claims the god Manitou made the mountain tremble *(montagne tremblante)* whenever human

beings interfered with nature. There's no danger of interference today—the mountain is surrounded by untamed national parkland, making it a top-notch site for year-round outdoor recreation. Though it's better known as a ski destination (see "Skiing in the Laurentians"), as the slopes thaw and the resulting mud disappears Mont-Tremblant offers a slew of summer sporting activities that include golf, boating, tennis, horseback riding, hiking, and more. The staff at the tourist office will help you arrange an afternoon of any of the activities listed above. If you don't mind getting dirty, one of the most exhilarating things you can do is take a 2-hour ATV tour with **Mont-Tremblant Guided ATV Tours** (☎ **888/738-1777**) for C$169. The price includes transport from the Mont-Tremblant activity center; a driver's license and C$2,000 security deposit are required) After roaring through the forests and streams surrounding Mont-Tremblant, you'll spend the entire evening trying to wipe the mud and smile off your face. *Tourisme de Mont-Tremblant, 5080 Montee Ryan. ☎ 819/425-2434. www.tourismemonttremblant.com. Prices vary according to activity. Open daily 8:30am–6pm (until 7pm Fri–Sat).*

A resort village at the base of Mont-Tremblant.

Festival des Arts

Started in 1991, the Festival des Art de St-Sauveur presents 10 days of dance and music performances at several venues around the lovely village of St-Sauveur each summer (usually in late July). Canadian and international troupes bring the small town to life with graceful ballet, breath-taking choral recitals, skilled stringed quartets, and intricately choreographed modern dance. Tickets, ranging in price from C$30 to C$60, can be hard to come by for some of the international acts without a little advance planning. But even if you don't see a performance, be sure to take advantage of the festival's free shows and workshops. You might partake in a kite-decorating workshop in the afternoon, and then catch a movie or concert later that night gratis. For information and/or reservations, call ☎ **450/227-9935** or check out **www.artssaintsauveur.com**.

In the morning, drive or hike to the foot of the mountain for your next two stops.

④ ★ **Lac Tremblant.** The largest of several lakes in the area, Lac Tremblant is a gorgeous stretch of water 16km (10 miles) long at the foot of Mont-Tremblant. Popular cruises take visitors on a soothing and educational trip around the lake, pointing out all sorts of interesting facts about the area, its history, and natural features. For a much more fulfilling experience, rent a kayak from **Centre Nautique Pierre Plouffe** (Beach & Tennis Club, Lac Tremblant, ☎ 819/681-5634; C$15 for 1 hr., C$26 for 2 hr.). Slowly paddle down the length of the peaceful lake and take the time to admire the rolling hills from your little vessel. *Croisières Mont-Tremblant (for cruises), 2810 chemin du village, Mont-Tremblant.* ☎ *819/425-1045. www.croisierestremblant.com. 70-min. narrated cruise costs C$15 adults, C$12 seniors, C$6 kids 6–15, and free for kids under 6. Open June–Oct; call for exact hours.*

A summer sail on Lac Tremblant is a peaceful and scenic way to spend an afternoon.

Skiing in the Laurentians

The snow may not be as soft as the powder you'll find in British Columbia and Alberta, but the ski slopes of Quebec's Laurentians are arguably the best in eastern North America. All the runs and trails here are well maintained and family friendly, with plenty of options for novices and beginners.

The most-visited of the region's major ski areas is Mont-Tremblant. For downhillers, the mountain—and its 94 runs and 13 lifts—is a dream. Cross-country skiers enjoy over 150km (93 miles) of both groomed and unmaintained trails. Thanks to its artificial snow, the season here can run from as early as November to as late as May. For information, ski trail maps, and up-to-date prices, consult **Tourisme de Mont-Tremblant,** 5080 Montée Ryan (☎ **800/ 322-2932** and 819/425-2434), which is open daily 9am to 5pm; or log on to **www.tourismemonttremblant.com**.

The Saint-Sauveur valley is also popular among Montréal weekenders. Saint-Sauveur (38 trails, five of which are double diamond–rated for experts) and Morin Heights (23 trails) are two villages that offer excellent skiing options. For skiing information in this area and pass pricing, call ☎ 450/227-4671, or check out **www.mssi.ca**.

⑤ Circuit Mont-Tremblant.
For many, the Laurentians offer an opportunity to escape the noise and stresses of traffic. Others come here just to see more of it. This full-fledged racetrack hosts all types of races, from GT tournaments to superbike championships. The track itself pales in comparison to the Grand Prix track in Montréal, but the surrounding forests and the backdrop of Mont-Tremblant drew racing legend Michael Schumacher to dub it "Little Nurburgring," after the famous German racetrack. Catching a race here can be very memorable, especially if you get seats along La Diable, the river bordering turn no. 4. It's a uniquely picturesque perch, and tickets are incredibly affordable when compared to those for the Grand Prix in Montréal. *Chemin Séguin.* ☎ *514/731-5717. www.le circuit.com. Tickets C$10–C$35. Most races take place June–mid-Sept.*

Skiers, snowboarders, and other winter sports enthusiasts flock to the Laurentians' world-class slopes.

Where to Stay

★ **Auberge Edelweiss** VAL DAVID This intimate inn is best known for its kitchen—once you've tasted the excellent French cuisine, you may never want to leave. The ultra-comfortable but simply furnished rooms, however, are nothing to sneeze at—some have fireplaces and Jacuzzis. *3050 chemin Doncaster.* ☎ *819/322-7800. www.ar-edelweiss.com. 13 units. Doubles C$190–C$240 (rates include breakfast & dinner). AE, MC, V.*

★★★ **Fairmont Mont-Tremblant** Mont-Tremblant This gem of a resort welcomes guests with a woodsy but modern lodge-style decor. Though the rooms are somewhat standard in style and amenities, the hotel sports an excellent range of recreational facilities and services. *3045 chemin de la Chapelle.* ☎ *800/441-1414 or 819/681-7000. www.fairmont.com. 314 units. Doubles C$539–C$769. AE, DC, DISC, MC, V.*

★★★ **Quintessence** Mont-Tremblant Many places in the region claim to be "luxury" resorts, but Quintessence truly whisks guests off to cloud nine. The all-suite property's comfortable accommodations have enormous, coma-inducing beds, and lots of bells and whistles in the bathrooms (heated floors, rain shower, etc.). *3004 chemin de la Chapelle.* ☎ *866/425-3400 or 819/425-3400. www.hotelquintessence.com. 30 units. Clagett's Cabin C$239–C$639; QSuite C$289–C$689. AE, DC, MC, V.*

Youth Hostel Tremblant Mont-Tremblant You'll sacrifice a little privacy and perhaps a little comfort at this ultra-affordable hostel, but you'll save quite a bit while meeting new ski buddies in your shared room. *2213 chemin du Village (Rte. 327).* ☎ *819/425-6008. www.hostelling Montréal.com. 240 beds. Single bed C$28, private rooms C$68. AE, MC, V.*

Where to Dine

kids Antipasto Mont-Tremblant *ITALIAN* This Italian cucina at the foot of Mont-Tremblant serves up oven-fired pizzas, seafood pastas, and lots of homey atmosphere. It's a surefire hit with kids, who love the railroad-related decorations in this converted train station. *855 rue de Saint-Jovite, St-Jovite.* ☎ *819/425-7580. Main courses C$12–C$33. AE, MC, V. Lunch & dinner daily.*

★ **Aux Truffes** Mont-Tremblant *FRENCH CONTEMPORARY* Aux Truffes offers a menu rife with well-thought-out and perfectly executed French cuisine complemented by an extensive wine list that's garnered praise from *Wine Spectator*. The

truffles are delectable. *3035 chemin de la Chapelle (Place Saint-Bernard).* ☎ *819/681-4544. www.auxtruffes.com. Main courses C$29–C$45. AE, MC, V. Dinner daily.*

The lodge-style lobby of the Fairmont Mont-Tremblant, one of the best resorts in the Laurentians.

Ottawa

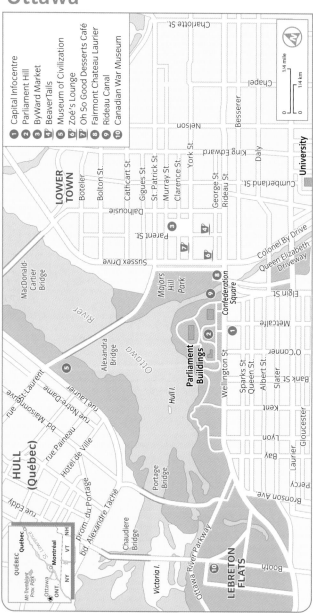

1 Capital Infocentre
2 Parliament Hill
3 ByWard Market
4 BeaverTails
5 Museum of Civilization
6 Zoë's Lounge
7 Oh So Good Desserts Café
8 Fairmont Chateau Laurier
9 Rideau Canal
10 Canadian War Museum

Set right between very Francophone Quebec and Anglophone Ontario, bilingual Ottawa is a hidden gem with an almost split personality—half government metropolis, half charming town. Two hours from Montréal, Canada's capital is the site of many of its national museums and heritage attractions, but it's also a walker's paradise with parks and gardens seemingly tucked in every corner. To see all of the city's attractions on a day trip is impossible, but this tour lets you sample its highlights. START: **To take full advantage of the city, your best bet is to rent a car and head out early from Montréal. Take Route 40 to the Trans Canada Highway west and into Ottawa (exit 118) (trip time: 2 hr.). Follow the red maple leaf signs into downtown and park in a municipal lot close to Parliament Hill.**

Travel Tip

Though distances are occasionally long, all of the stops on this tour are reachable on foot. So you can theoretically park your car and hoof it in spring and summer (the best times to take this side trip). Walking is truly the best way to see Ottawa's core. That said, if your mobility is limited or you have little kids along, you should drive to the Museum of Civilization and the Canadian War Museum. Both offer inexpensive short-term parking for visitors.

Ottawa's famed Parliament Hill is dominated by the central Peace Tower.

❶ Capital Infocentre. It's loaded with brochures (pick up the worthwhile self-guided walking tour booklet for Parliament Hill), maps, and other tourist information. There's a short video presentation on the city's major attractions, and a friendly and expert staff is on hand to answer questions. ⏱ *20 min. 90 Wellington St.* ☎ *613/239-5000 or 800/465-1867. www.ottawatourism.ca. Daily mid-May–Labour Day 8:30am–5pm; Sept–mid-May 9am–5pm. Closed Christmas, Dec 26, and New Year's Day.*

❷ ★★ Parliament Hill. It's not quite Britain's Palace of Westminster (upon which it was based), but Parliament Hill's neo-Gothic architecture is ultra-photogenic, and the central

Peace Tower (with its enormous clock face) does remind you of Big Ben. Composed of the East, West, and Centre blocks, the Hill is home to the Canadian legislature. If you arrive early enough in Ottawa (summer only), check out the Hill's colorful Changing of the Guard—it's less touristy than its London counterpart. Afterwards, stroll the lovely grounds. If you do nothing else, walk behind the Centre Block for a fabulous view of the Ottawa River. ***Note:*** You can take timed-ticket tours of the Parliament building interiors, but scheduling issues make this a time-wasting option on a day trip. ⏱ *30 min.–1 hr. Wellington St. www.parl.gc.ca. Free admission. Changing of Guard 10am late June–late Aug only.*

Take in the pageantry of the changing of the guard at Parliament Hill in summer. See p. 139.

❸ ★ ByWard Market. The charming ByWard Market, established in 1826 by Ottawa-founder Col. John By, is the oldest continuing farmer's market in Canada. Set along cobblestone streets and courtyards just a block behind the Chateau Laurier, this bustling marketplace is the perfect place to pick up picnic supplies and local crafts. You can browse the market stalls and boutiques, have a meal at one of the many cafes, grab a beer at one of the bars or pubs, or just people-watch. *Bounded by Cathcart, Rideau, Cumberland, and Sussex sts. www.byward-market. com. Individual vendor hours vary, though most shops are open daily 9:30am–6pm. Closed Christmas and New Year's Day.*

❹ ★★★ kids BeaverTails sells the yummy BeaverTail—a large, sweet, whole-wheat pastry shaped (you guessed it) like a beaver's tail. This local favorite comes in many delicious flavors, though you can't go wrong with the traditional version topped with cinnamon and sugar. *69 George St. ☎ 613/241-6321. www.beavertailsinc.com. $.*

❺ ★★★ kids Museum of Civilization. Canada's most visited museum is housed in an architectural wonder designed by Douglas Cardinal (who also did the Smithsonian's National Museum of the American Indian). The First Nations displays (including the world's largest indoor collection of totem poles) are first-rate. Other highlights include the Canadian Postal Museum (who knew stamps could be so entertaining?); the amazing Canada Hall, which lets you walk through exhibits charting 1,000 years of Canadian social history; a fabulous interactive children's museum; and an IMAX theater (separate fee). The two genuine Canadian Mounties who pose for snapshots are quite the hot ticket as well. ⏱ 2–3 hr. 100 Laurier St. ☎ 819/776-7000. www.civilization.ca. Admission C$10 adults, C$7 seniors, and C$4 kids 3–12. Discount ticket combo packages including Canadian Museum of War and IMAX films available. Free admission July 1. May–Sept Fri–Wed 9am–6pm, Thurs 9am–9pm; Oct–Apr Tues–Sun 9am–5pm, Thurs till 9pm.

ByWard Market, the oldest farmer's market in Canada.

The elegant and ever-so-civilized (dress accordingly) **6** **Zoé's Lounge** is *the* place to take afternoon tea in Ottawa. Feast on finger sandwiches, delicious teacakes, incredibly good scones, and one of 13 loose teas (wheeled to you for inspection on an antique tea cart). If the prices (C$24–C$49, depending on the option selected) seem high, they are almost half of what you'd pay for a comparable experience in London, but no less authentic. *Tip:* Ask for a table with a view over Rideau Street and you'll be treated to great people-watching. *Inside the Fairmont Chateau Laurier, 1 Rideau St.* 613/241-1425. ext. 58. *Reservations are a must. $$.* For a less formal afternoon snack, try **7** **kids** **Oh So Good Desserts Café,** where you can pig out on huge portions of scrumptious cakes, cookies, and pies. *25 York St.* 708/241-8028. *$.*

8 ★ **Fairmont Chateau Laurier.** Modeled on a 16th-century French chateau (its photogenic turrets and spires are a fixture of the downtown Ottawa skyline), this landmark hotel debuted in 1912 and has been Ottawa's top place to stay ever since. A stroll through the hotel's elegant public rooms (evocative of the early 1900s) is worthwhile, and an interesting photo gallery on the hotel's ground floor details the rich history of the property. You might even spot the hotel's resident ghost. The Chateau Laurier's builder, Charles Melville Hays, may never have set

The iconic Fairmont Chateau Laurier, an Ottawa landmark, opened in 1912.

foot in his finished creation (he was traveling to the hotel's grand opening aboard the RMS *Titanic* and went down with the ill-fated ship), but his spirit has been spotted here on several occasions. 🕑 *15 min.* *1 Rideau St.* 613/241-1414. *Free admission to photo gallery. Most public rooms open daily, round-the-clock.*

9 **Rideau Canal.** This historic 201km (125-mile) waterway runs through the center of Ottawa before making its way to Kingston, Ontario. It's the oldest canal system in North America and great for boating or strolling in summer. Though the path along the canal makes for a scenic walk (and some good photo-ops) year-round, it's especially picturesque in winter, when the canal turns into the world's largest skating rink. Be sure to take in the unique lock system that allows ships to pass through to the Ottawa River. *Locks adjacent to Fairmont Chateau Laurier, 1 Rideau St.* www.rideau-info.com/canal. *See website for boating and lock fees and hours.*

A First Nations artifact from the Museum of Civilization.

Rideau Who?

Many visitors assume, wrongly, that the Rideau Canal (and the seemingly endless number of other places in Ottawa that bear the name Rideau) was named for some historic personage. In actuality, as amused locals like to point out, the name game started in 1613, when explorer Samuel de Champlain thought the waterfall that emptied the canal's waters into the Ottawa River looked like his living room curtains (*rideau* is French for curtain) and named it accordingly.

⑩ ★★★ **Canadian War Museum.** I have only a superficial interest in military history, but this exceptional museum (opened in 2005) is one of my favorite experiences in the city and truly unique. The museum examines the impact of war on a personal, national, and global level through the use of artifacts, art, interactive displays, a huge number of military vehicles and assorted weaponry, and video presentations. It's educational and emotionally affecting no matter what your nationality. It's also an architectural wonder—a lot of careful planning went into the environmentally sensitive structure, which was

A display of aircraft and weaponry at the impressive Canadian Museum of War.

A system of 47 locks allows ships to pass through the Rideau Canal to the Ottawa River. See p. 141.

designed so that each year at 11am on Remembrance Day (Nov 11), the sun illuminates the headstone of Canada's Unknown Soldier in the museum's Memorial Hall. And if you look at the North Fin on the exterior, you'll find the words LEST WE FORGET inscribed in Morse code (in true Ottawa fashion, it's spelled out in both French and English). ⏱ *1½ hr. 1 Vimy Place. 5621 or 819/776-8600. www.warmuseum.ca. Admission C$10 adults, C$7 seniors, C$4 kids 4 to 12, C$22 families; admission is half-price Sun and free Thurs 4–9pm. Discount combination ticket packages with Museum of Civilization available. Open Oct–Apr daily 9am–5pm; May–Sept daily 9am–6pm; year-round Thurs until 9pm.* ●

Before You Go

Government Tourist Offices

In the U.S.: The main Québec tourist information office is at Délégation générale du Québec, 1 Rockefeller Plaza, 26th Floor, New York, NY 10020 (☎ **212/397-0200**). For a list of branch offices in the U.S., check the agency's website at **www. Québecusa.org**. **In the U.K.:** Contact Délégation générale du Québec, 59 Pall Mall, London SW1Y 5JH, England (☎ **44-207/766-5900**; www. Québec.org.uk).

The province also has a large office that's open to the public in Montréal at 1255 rue Peel.

The Best Times to Go

The summer months—June through August—may be hot and humid, but they're also when Montréal is at its busiest and you'll pay the most for a hotel room. In spring it may be easier to get accommodations and the weather may be more comfortable, but you'll miss out on the city's big festivals. September and October are less hectic months and they're the perfect time for autumn hikes to glimpse the region's beautiful fall foliage. Winter in Montréal is often brutally cold and snowy, but hotel rooms can be hard to find from Christmas to New Year's, and during the city's top winter festivals. The worst times to visit are early spring and late fall, when the weather can get iffy and not much is happening in town.

Festivals & Special Events

JAN. **La Fête des Neiges** (Snow Festival; ☎ **514/872-4537**; www.fetedesneiges.com) is the city's premier winter festival and features outdoor events such as harness racing, barrel jumping, ice sculpting, snowshoeing, skating, and cross-country skiing.

FEB. Top events at the **Montréal Highlights Festival** (☎ **888/477-9955**; www.Montréalhighlights. com) include nearly 200 culinary competitions and wine tastings, special museum exhibitions and multimedia light shows, and classical and pop concerts by international musical greats.

MAY. Admission to most of the city's museums is free to all visitors on **Montréal Museums Day** (☎ **877/266-5687**; www.museesMontréal. org); there are even free buses to get you from place to place.

JUNE. The **Montréal Bike Fest** (☎ **800/567-8356**; www.velo.qc.ca) brings thousands of cyclists to the city for numerous races of varying degrees of length and difficulty. Around the same time, **Mutek** (☎ **514/392-9251**; www.mutek.ca) celebrates everything electronica with concerts and performances by an international cast of DJ's and artists. About 70 theater groups perform in highly esoteric productions staged along boulevard St-Laurent in the **Saint-Ambroise Montréal Fringe Festival** (☎ **514/849-3378**; www.Montréalfringe.ca).

JULY. Hordes of sightseers and music fans make the **Montréal International Jazz Festival** (☎ **800/361-4595** or 514/790-1245; www. Montréaljazzfest.com) one of the most exciting in the world. Improvised jazz solos are replaced by improvisational comedy at the **Festival Juste pour Rire** (☎ **888/244-3155** or 514/790-4242; www.hahaha. com), where big names in comedy aim to keep the city in stitches. The 30-minute shows, with music, staged

MONTRÉAL'S AVERAGE MONTHLY TEMPERATURES (°F/°C)

	JAN	FEB	MAR	APR	MAY	JUNE
High (°F)	22	24	34	50	65	74
(°C)	−6	−4	1	10	18	23
Low (°F)	8	10	21	35	47	57
(°C)	−13	−12	−6	2	8	14
Avg. Rainfall (in./mm)	2.8/70	2.4/60	2.8/72	3.0/76	3.0/76	3.3/84

	JULY	AUG	SEPT	OCT	NOV	DEC
High (°F)	78	77	67	55	40	27
(°C)	26	25	19	13	4	−3
Low (°F)	62	60	52	41	29	14
(°C)	17	16	11	5	−2	−10
Avg. Rainfall (in./mm)	3.5/90	3.6/94	3.6/91	3.0/78	3.7/93	3.2/82

for the **International Fireworks Competition** (www.lemondialsaq.com) light up the skies above Île Ste-Hélène. A parade, concerts, parties, and art shows mark the gay and lesbian community's annual pride celebration, **Diver/Cité** (☎ 514/285-4011; www.diverscite.org).

AUG. Some 500 indoor and outdoor screenings take place over the 12-day **World Film Festival** (☎ 514/848-3883; www.ffm-Montréal.org), which isn't as gaudy or as media-heavy as Cannes, but it's taken almost as seriously. If you can't buy tickets to a showing in the Cinema Imperial, walk south a couple of blocks to Place des Arts for a free, outdoor film.

SEPT. It's the perfect time of year to view the **fall foliage** in the city's parks and the surrounding region, especially the Laurentians (p 132).

OCT. During the **Black & Blue Festival** (☎ 514/875-7026; www.bbcm.org), 7 days of gay benefit parties, art shows, and cultural events are held at various locations throughout the city. Screenings of experimental and controversial films, as well as forums on trends in cinema, mark the **Festival du Nouveau Cinéma** (☎ 514/847-1242; www.nouveaucinema.ca).

NOV. The long-running **Image + Nation** (www.image-nation.org) gay and lesbian film festival screens innovative and experimental fare.

The Weather

It's a city of extremes when it comes to the weather. There's really only two seasons in Montréal: an oppressively humid and hot summer and a bitterly cold winter. About 2 weeks of pleasant spring and fall take place between the two major seasons.

Useful Websites

- **www.moremontreal.com**: An extensive collection of links to various websites relating to Montréal, with information on everything from hotels to local dance troupes to general facts about the city.

- **www.tourisme-montreal.org**: This slick site offers views of Montréal from webcams set up in different parts of town. You'll also find information on upcoming festivals and events.

- **www.admtl.com**: Montréal-Trudeau Airport's site is a cache of important information for travelers arriving and departing from the city's main airport. Special alerts and information about services at the airport can be found here.

- **www.montrealmirror.com**: The website for Montréal's best weekly alternative publication displays the same concert listings and entertainment articles as the print version.

- **www.stm.info**: Montréal's public transportation system website posts service interruptions, as well as detailed route maps of its bus and Métro lines.

- **www.vieux.montreal.qc.ca**: An excellent resource for information about all the sites in Vieux-Montréal. You'll also find historical information about area landmarks and the region in general.

- **http://montrealplus.ca**: This site's Yellow Pages–style listings include small yet useful descriptions of various businesses—clubs, restaurants, shops, and more—in Montréal.

Cellphones

If you have a wireless system that covers both the U.S. and Canada—Verizon is one—you won't have to rent a cellphone, though you might have to upgrade your account temporarily to be able to use your phone in Canada. Call your phone company and ask for your options and the pricing schedule. Unfortunately, per-minute charges can be high.

Otherwise, renting a phone is a good idea. While you can rent a phone from any number of overseas sites, including kiosks at airports and at car-rental agencies, we suggest renting the phone before you leave home. North Americans can rent one before leaving home from **InTouch USA** (☎ **800/872-7626;** www.intouchglobal.com) or **RoadPost** (☎ **888/290-1606** or 905/272-5665; www.roadpost.com).

Car Rentals

If you're arriving in town by train or plane, you won't actually need a car in Montréal unless you plan on taking day trips outside the city limits. Even then you should wait to rent until you're actually ready to head out. Free parking can be scarce and gasoline (petrol) is more expensive than it is in the United States (though cheaper than what you'll pay elsewhere).

If you still want to rent, all the major U.S. car-rental companies are represented in Montréal. You'll find rental agencies in the downtown area as well as at Pierre-Eliot-Trudeau airport. In addition to the big names, **Via Route** (**www.viaroute.com**) is an excellent Canadian company that rents everything from compacts to small trucks. It has several branch offices in Montréal, including one at 3700 Ste-Catherine est (☎ **514/521-8155**).

The best online deals are usually found at rental-car company websites, although all the major online travel agencies also offer rental-car reservations services. Priceline (www.priceline.com) and Hotwire (www.hotwire.com) work well for rental cars, too; the only "mystery" is which major rental company you get, and for most travelers the difference between Hertz, Avis, and Budget is negligible. (If you do have a preferred rental car company, Priceline now allows you to shop and compare between companies.)

Getting **There**

By Plane

Montréal's main airport is **Aéroport International Pierre-Elliot-Trudeau de Montréal** (☎ 800/465-1213 or 514/394-7377; www.admtl.com), known better as Montréal-Trudeau Airport. It's 23km (14 miles) southwest of downtown Montréal, and is served by nearly 50 major airlines. The only other area airport, **Aéroport Mirabel,** 55km (34 miles) northwest of the city, receives only freight and charter flights.

A **taxi** will get you from the airport to downtown Montréal for a flat rate of C$31; trip time is 30 minutes to an hour, depending on traffic.

A cheaper transport method is **L'Aérobus** (☎ 514/842-2281), which shuttles between the airport and the Central Bus Station at 505 bd. de Maisonneuve est. One-way fares are C$13 adults, C$12 seniors, and C$9.25 children. Free minibuses take passengers from the terminal to 60 major hotels. Schedules change frequently, but buses usually operate daily every 20 to 30 minutes from Montréal-Trudeau between 4:45am and 11:45pm; trip time from the airport to the bus station is about 40 minutes, depending on traffic.

By Car

Many visitors from the mid-Atlantic and New England regions of the United States (as well as the eastern sections of Canada) prefer to drive to Montréal. **Interstate 87** runs due north from New York City to link up with Canada's **Autoroute 15** at the border, and the entire 644km (400-mile) journey is on expressways. Likewise, from Boston, **I-93** north joins **I-89** just south of Concord, New Hampshire. At White River Junction there is a choice between continuing on I-89 to Lake Champlain, crossing the lake by roads and bridges to join I-87 and Canada Autoroute 15 north, or picking up **I-91** at White River Junction to go due north toward Sherbrooke, Québec. At the border, I-91 becomes Canada **Route 55** and joins Canada **Route 10** west to Montréal. The **Trans-Canada Highway,** which connects both ends of the country, runs right through Montréal.

From Boston to Montréal is about 515km (320 miles); from Toronto, 540km (335 miles); from Ottawa, 190km (118 miles).

By Train

Montréal is a major rail hub on Canada's **ViaRail** (☎ 888/842-7245; www.viarail.ca) network, and welcomes trains from many locations in the country. From the U.S., **Amtrak** (☎ 800/872-7245; www.amtrak.com) runs only one train to Montréal; its no-frills but scenic *Adirondack* travels north from Washington and New York. The trip usually takes 10½ hours, but long delays at the border can easily make this a 13-hour trek. All trains arrive at **Gare Centrale,** at 895 rue de la Gauchetière ouest (☎ 514/989-2626), from which you can connect to the Bonaventure Métro station via the "underground city" shopping complex.

By Bus

Montréal's main bus terminal is the **Terminus Voyageur** on 505 bd. De Maisonneuve est (☎ 514/842-2281), which is located at the Berri-Uqam Métro stop. **Greyhound** (☎ 800/229-9494 or 514/843-8495; www.greyhound.com) operates routes from Boston and New York to Montréal, while **Adirondack Trailways** (☎ 800/858-8555) shuttles between Montréal and New York. The trip from Boston takes about 8 hours; from

New York City, it takes 9 hours. The seats may be a bit more cramped and the views a little less scenic than what you'll get on a train, but those traveling with minimal luggage should forgo the train and use the bus.

Though the cost is similar, the bus makes fewer stops en route and you'll get through Customs much faster, making the bus trip anywhere from an hour to 3 hours faster than taking Amtrak.

Getting Around

By Public Transportation
For speed and economy, nothing beats Montréal's **Métro system,** which is run by the **Société de Transport de Montréal** or **STM** (☎ **514/288-2627;** www.stm.info). The underground subway system, modeled after the one in Paris, consists of four color-coded lines, and is clean, reliable, and simple to use. Stations are marked by blue-and-white signs that show a circle enclosing a down-pointing arrow. Buy tickets at the booth in any station, or from a convenience store. Slip your ticket into the slot in the turnstile to enter the system. Take a transfer (correspondence) from the machine just inside the turnstiles of every station; it allows transfers from a train to a bus at any other Métro station for no additional fare. You must take the transfer ticket at the station where you first enter the system. Single rides cost C$2.50, a strip of six tickets costs C$12, and a weekly unlimited pass costs C$19.

The Métro does have a few downsides: It's not available 24/7, and it has very limited accessibility for those with mobility problems. The orange, green, and yellow Métro lines run from about 5:30am to 12:30am (until 11:30pm on Sat), and the blue line runs from 5:30am to 11:10pm. Night owls out past closing time must make do with taxis or the city's bus system.

City buses, also run by STM, aren't as efficient as the Métro,

though they do run to places that the Métro doesn't stop. Some routes also run late at night (often on a limited schedule), long after the Métro's shut down for the evening. The cost is the same as for the Métro; if you want to pay in cash instead of using a ticket, you need to have exact change. If you start a trip on the bus and want to transfer to the Métro, ask the bus driver for a transfer ticket.

Tip: Ask the ticket collector at any Métro station for a free map of the Island of Montréal's entire transit system, which includes all bus routes. Routes are also usually printed on bus stop signs, though drivers are friendly enough to help you find your way if you get lost.

By Taxi
There's no single general taxi company in the city, and taxis tend to come in all shapes, sizes, and colors. As a result, the only way to distinguish a taxi from a normal car is the illuminated sign on its roof. Taxis line up outside most large hotels or can be hailed on the street. Members of hotel and restaurant staffs can also call cabs, many of which are dispatched by radio.

The meter starts running at C$3.15 and climbs in increments of C$1.45 after each kilometer. It's C$.55 for each minute of waiting time, but a flat fee of C$31 is all that's required to get you from anywhere in the downtown area to the airport. Tip about 10% to 15% of the total tab.

Note that Montréal taxi drivers can range in temperament from sullen cranks to unstoppable chatterboxes. Some know the city well, others have sketchy knowledge and may not speak good English. It's always a good idea to have your destination written down—with cross streets—to show your driver.

By Car

Though the city's ideal for walking, and public transportation is efficient, if you want to drive, you shouldn't have problems getting through the streets of Montréal. Prudent drivers should avoid the busy Rue Ste-Catherine and opt for Boulevard Rene Levesque if you want to travel east-west through downtown. Otherwise, you might only have trouble shifting into gear on some of the incredibly steep streets (such as Rue University and Rue Peel, near Av. des Pins). All familiar rules apply, though turning right on red in the city is prohibited.

On Foot

For a metropolis, it's a surprisingly easy city to navigate with just a pair of sneakers. Certain parts of the Plateau (Av. Prince Arthur between Bd. St-Laurent and Av. Laval, and Place Jacques Cartier) prohibit cars altogether. With the existence of the underground city, exploring Montréal by foot might be the easiest way to access some of the sights. Be careful in the wintertime, however. Sidewalks can be extremely icy and nighttime strolls can be interrupted by loud sidewalk vehicles that shovel snow to the curbs.

Fast **Facts**

APARTMENT RENTALS **Louer.com** (☎ **866/455-6837** or 514/223-4444; www.louer.com) is one of the best sites for finding apartment rentals in Quebec. **moreMontréal** (www. moremontreal.com/apartments) is another excellent resource that publishes maps and detailed information on each of its apartments.

AREA CODES   Montréal's area code is 514.

ATMS/CASHPOINTS   The **Cirrus** (☎ **800/424-7787**; www.mastercard. com) and **PLUS** (☎ **800/843-7587**; www.visa.com) networks span the globe; look at the back of your bank card to see which network you're on, then call or check online for automated teller machine (ATM) locations in Montréal (they're found all over the city, so you shouldn't have trouble finding one).

Be sure you know your personal identification number (PIN) before you leave home and be sure to find out your daily withdrawal limit before you depart. Also keep in mind that many banks impose a fee every time a card is used at a different bank's ATM, and that fee can be higher for international transactions (up to $5 or more) than for domestic ones.

Note: Some small establishments in Montréal won't take credit cards, so it's always wise to carry a small amount of cash on you.

BABYSITTERS   Many Montréal hotels offer some form of babysitting service. If not, your hotel's concierge should be able to help you find a reliable babysitter.

BANKS   Banks are generally open from 9am to 4pm Monday to Friday.

Most major Canadian banks have branches on either rue Sherbrooke or rue Ste-Catherine.

B&BS The **Downtown B&B Network,** 3458 av. Laval (☎ 514/289-9749; www.bbmontreal.qc.ca) rents over 40 rooms in excellent bed-and-breakfasts located in four different downtown neighborhoods.

BIKE RENTALS The best place to rent a bicycle is **VéloMontréal,** located at 3880 Rachel est (☎ 514/259-7272; www.velomontreal.com). It's open 9am to 6pm Monday to Wednesday, 9am to 7pm Thursday to Friday, 10am to 5pm on Saturday, and noon to 5pm on Sunday. The store rents out Fuji hybrid and mountain bikes for a few hours or for a few days. Prices start at C$15 for 2 hours and climb all the way up to $120 for a week.

BUSINESS HOURS Hardcore shoppers will be disappointed to find out that most shops operate only from 9 or 10am to 6pm Monday through Wednesday. They can make up lost time on Thursdays and Fridays, however, when stores generally stay open from 9am to 9pm. On Saturdays stores are open from 9am to 5pm. Sunday store hours are more limited, usually from noon to 5pm.

CONSULATES & EMBASSIES Most embassies and consulates are located in the Canadian national capital of Ottawa (p 38). Three English-speaking countries do maintain consulates in Montréal. The **Consulate General of the United States** is at 1155 rue St-Alexandre (☎ 514/398-9695). The **United Kingdom** has a consulate general at 1000 rue de la Gauchetière ouest, Suite 4200 (☎ 514/866-5863). **Ireland** has a consulate general at Concordia University, 1590 Dr. Penfield Ave. (☎ 514/848-7389).

CURRENCY EXCHANGE You can exchange currency at many locations (train station, bus station, hotels) in downtown Montréal. Rue Ste-Catherine is littered with currency exchange booths that deal in all forms of world currency. Some Montréal establishments will accept U.S. money, but don't expect a great exchange rate—some places simply take it as the equivalent of Canadian money.

CUSTOMS Normal baggage and personal possessions should be no problem, but tobacco and alcoholic beverages face import restrictions. Travelers 18 and over are allowed to bring in 50 cigars, 200 cigarettes, and 200 grams of loose tobacco, and either 1.14 liters of liquor, 1.5 liters of wine, or a curiously generous case (24 cans or bottles) of beer.

For more detailed information concerning Customs regulations, write to the **Canada Customs Office,** 400 place d'Youville, 2nd Floor, Montréal, PQ H2Y 2C2 (☎ 514/283-2949 or 514/283-2959); or check out the Customs website at **www.ccra-adrc.gc.ca.**

DENTISTS "See Emergencies," below.

DINING It's a good idea, and an expected courtesy, to make a reservation if you wish to dine at one of the city's top restaurants. Unlike in larger American and European cities, reserving a day or two in advance is usually sufficient. A hotel concierge can make your reservation, but do note that most restaurant hosts will immediately speak English if they sense a caller doesn't speak French. Dress codes are all but nonexistent, except in a handful of luxury restaurants, but adults who show up in T-shirts and jeans will feel uncomfortably out of place at fashionable Montréal's better establishments.

To dine for less, try to have your main meal at lunch (most places start serving at 11:30am). Another option is to try one of the ubiquitous table d'hôte (fixed-price) meals, where an entire two- to four-course meal, often with a beverage, can be had for little more than the price of an a la carte main course alone. And because imported alcohol-based beverages are heavily taxed, to save a little, stick to Canadian beers and wine (especially the region's dessert ice wines) with your meals.

DOCTORS   "See Emergencies," below.

DRUGSTORES   A pharmacy is called a *pharmacie*, a drugstore is a *droguerie*. Various pharmacies can be found in the city, especially in downtown Montréal. An important chain is **Pharmaprix.** Its branch at 5122 chemin Queen Mary (☎ **514/738-8464**) is open 24 hours a day, 365 days a year, and has a fairly convenient location.

ELECTRICITY   Like the United States, Canada uses 110–120 volts AC (60 cycles) compared to 220–240 volts AC (50 cycles) in most of Europe, Australia, and New Zealand. If your small appliances use 220–240 volts, you'll need a 110-volt transformer and a plug adapter with two flat parallel pins to operate them here. Downward converters that change 220–240 volts to 110–120 volts are difficult to find in Canada, so bring one with you.

EMERGENCIES   For general emergencies dial ☎ **911** for the police, an ambulance, or firefighters.

The **Hôpital Royal Victoria,** 687 av. des Pins ouest (☎ **514/934-1934**), behind McGill University, is where most ambulances and walk-ins from downtown go for an emergency room visit. **Hôpital de Montréal pour Enfants** (☎ **514/412-4400**) is a children's hospital with a poison center.

For emergency dental visits call ☎ **514/288-8888;** call ☎ **514/342-4444** for the 24-hour dental clinic.

EVENT LISTINGS   The *Montréal Mirror* and the *Hour* are great publications that print concert, theater, and film listings for the city. They're widely available for free in restaurants, hotels, shops, and cafes.

FAMILY TRAVEL   Look for items tagged with a "kids" icon in this book.

Montréal offers an abundance of family-oriented activities, many of them outdoors, even in winter. Dog sledding, watersports, river cruises, and frequent festivals and fireworks displays are among the family-friendly attractions. Many museums make special efforts to address children's interests and enthusiasms.

Familyhostel (☎ 800/733-9753; www.learn.unh.edu/familyhostel) takes the whole family, including kids ages 8 to 15, on moderately priced domestic and international learning vacations. Lectures, fields trips, and sightseeing are guided by a team of academics.

Recommended family travel Internet sites include **Family Travel Forum** (www.familytravelforum.com), a comprehensive site that offers customized trip planning; **Family Travel Network** (www.familytravelnetwork.com), an award-winning site that offers travel features, deals, and tips; **Traveling Internationally with Your Kids** (www.travelwithyourkids.com), a comprehensive site offering sound advice for long-distance and international travel with children; and **Family Travel Files** (www.thefamilytravelfiles.com), which offers an online magazine and a directory of off-the-beaten-path tours and tour operators for families.

GAY & LESBIAN TRAVELERS   In Montréal, gay and lesbian travelers head straight to the Gay Village, lying primarily along Rue Ste-Catherine est between Rue St-Hubert and Rue Papineau, where there are numerous meeting spots, shops, bars, and clubs. **Gay Line** (☎ **514/866-5090** or 888/505-1010 outside the 514 area code; www.gayline.qc.ca) describes current events and activities in English, daily from 7 to 10pm. **Gay-Info** (☎ 514/768-0199) helps the Anglophone gay and lesbian community with various problems or concerns. It's open Fridays and Saturdays from 7:30am to 10:30pm.

Two websites that may prove useful are **www.gaywired.com** and **www.fugues.com**. The latter is a leisure guide to gay life in Montréal and other Québec cities; you can find the printed version in bars and hotels in and around the Village. Additional information is available at **The Village Tourist Information Centre** at 576 rue Ste-Catherine est opposite the Berri-UQAM Métro station (☎ **514/522-1885;** www. infogayvillage.com).

HOLIDAYS   Public holidays include: New Year's Day (Jan 1); Good Friday (last Fri of Mar or first Fri of Apr); Easter Monday (Mon following Good Friday); Victoria Day (Mon preceding May 25); National Day (June 24); Canada Day (July 1); Labour Day (1st Mon of Sept); Thanksgiving Day (2nd Mon of Oct); Remembrance Day (Nov 11); Christmas (Dec 25); Boxing Day (Dec 26).

INSURANCE   **For U.S. Visitors:** Check your existing insurance policies and credit card coverage before you buy travel insurance. You may already be covered for canceled tickets, lost luggage, or medical expenses. The cost of travel insurance varies widely, depending on the cost and length of your trip, your age, your health, and the type of trip you're taking, but expect to pay between 5% and 8% of the vacation itself.

Trip-cancellation insurance helps you get your money back if you have to back out of a trip, if you

have to go home early, or if your travel supplier goes bankrupt. Allowed reasons for cancellation can range from sickness to natural disasters to the State Department declaring your destination unsafe for travel. (Insurers usually won't cover vague fears, though.) In this unstable world, trip-cancellation insurance is a good buy if you're getting tickets well in advance. Insurance policy details vary, so read the fine print—and especially make sure that your airline is on the list of carriers covered in case of bankruptcy. For information, contact one of the following insurers: **Access America** (☎ **866/807-3982;** www. accessamerica.com), **Travel Guard International** (☎ **800/826-4919;** www.travelguard.com), **Travel Insured International** (☎ **800/243-3174;** www.travelinsured.com), or **Travelex Insurance Services** (☎ **888/457-4602;** www.travelex-insurance.com).

Medical Insurance: For travel overseas, most health plans (including Medicare and Medicaid) do not provide coverage, and the ones that do often require you to pay for services upfront and reimburse you only after you return home. Medical treatment in Canada isn't free for foreigners, and hospitals make you pay your bills at the time of service. They'll send you a refund after you've returned home and filed the necessary paperwork. In a worst-case scenario, there's the high cost of emergency evacuation. If you require additional medical insurance, try **MEDEX Assistance** (☎ **410/453-6300;** www.medexassist.com) or **Travel Assistance International** (☎ **800/821-2828;** www.travelassistance.com—for general information on services, call the company's Worldwide Assistance Services, Inc., at ☎ 800/777-8710).

Insurance for British Travelers:
Most big travel agents offer their
own insurance and will probably try
to sell you their package when you
book a holiday. Think before you
sign. **Britain's Consumers' Association** recommends that you insist on
seeing the policy and reading the
fine print before buying travel insurance. **The Association of British
Insurers** (☎ 020/7600-3333; www.
abi.org.uk) gives advice by phone
and publishes *Holiday Insurance*, a
free guide to policy provisions and
prices. You might also shop around
for better deals: Try **Columbus
Direct** (☎ 020/7375-0011; www.
columbusdirect.net).

Lost-Luggage Insurance: On international flights (including U.S. portions of international trips), baggage
is limited to approximately $9.07
per pound, up to approximately
$635 per checked bag. If you plan to
check items more valuable than the
standard liability, see if your valuables are covered by your home-
owner's policy, or get baggage
insurance as part of your comprehensive travel-insurance package.
Don't buy insurance at the airport,
as it's invariably overpriced. Be sure
to take any valuables or irreplace-
able items with you in your carry-on
luggage, as many valuables (including books, money, and electronics)
aren't covered by airline policies.

If your luggage is lost, immediately file a lost-luggage claim at the
airport, detailing the luggage con-
tents. For most airlines, you must
report delayed, damaged, or lost
baggage within 4 hours of arrival.

INTERNET ACCESS   Many cafes and
hotels offer Internet access, but
CyberGround NetCafe, 3672 bd.
St-Laurent (☎ **514/842-1726**), is
one of the better places to access
your e-mail and surf the Web.

LIQUOR LAWS   Wine and beer can be
bought in groceries or the corner

dep (short for *dépanneur,* the
Québec equivalent of a convenience
store). Hard liquor and spirits are
regulated by the *Québec Société des
Alcools* (look for maroon signs with
the acronym SAQ all around the city).
Note: Canadian beers are much
stronger than their American coun-
terparts; even American beers such
as Budweiser contain more alcohol in
Canada than they do in the U.S.

The legal drinking age in the
province is 18. Liquor is sold every
day of the week in SAQ stores. Bars
stop pouring drinks at 3am, but usually stay open until 4am.

LOST PROPERTY   Be sure to tell all of
your credit card companies as soon
as you discover your wallet has
been lost or stolen, and file a report
at the nearest police precinct. For
this reason, keep a list of both credit
card numbers and the emergency
telephone numbers of the companies in a separate place. (It should
be listed on the back of the card.)
Your credit card company or insurer
may require a police report number
or record of the loss. They may be
able to wire you a cash advance
immediately or deliver an emergency card in a day or two.

If you lose something on the
Métro, call the **STCUM info-line** at
☎ **514/786-4636** and follow the
prompts to report your missing
belongings.

MAIL & POSTAGE   All mail posted in
Canada must bear Canadian stamps.
Within Canada, letters cost C49¢,
letters to the United States are C80¢,
and they're C$1.40 anywhere else.
Postal cards cost the same as a
first-class letter. These prices are
increased by the imposition of a C8¢
sales tax on a first-class stamp.

The main Montréal post office
is at 1250 rue University (☎ **514/
846-5401**). It's open 8am to 6pm
Monday through Friday. In Vieux

Montréal, there's a branch at 155 rue St-Jacques. To find a post office nearest your hotel, check out **www. canadapost.ca**.

MONEY Canadian money comes in graduated denominations of dollars and cents. New bills featuring tougher security measures, bolder colors, and more modern designs are being introduced into circulation, though the dollar and two-dollar denominations are in the form of coins, nicknamed the Loonie and the Toonie respectively.

At press time, the Canadian dollar was worth about 89¢ in U.S. currency and 67 British pence, give or take a couple of points' daily variation. The best way to get cash is through an ATM or cashpoint (see "ATMs/Cashpoints," above). Credit cards are accepted at almost all shops, restaurants, and hotels, but you should always keep some cash on hand for incidentals.

NEWSPAPERS & MAGAZINES The local English-language newspaper, the *Montréal Gazette* (**www.Montréal gazette.com**), is an excellent publication that covers local, national, and international news. Canada's national newspaper is the *Globe and Mail*. Both papers can be found at newsstands or at **Multimags,** 3550 bd. St-Laurent, a store with an excellent selection of international newspapers and magazines.

PARKING It can be difficult to park for free on the heavily trafficked streets of downtown Montréal, but there are plenty of metered spaces, with varying hourly rates. (Look around before walking off without paying. Meters are set well back from the curb so they won't be buried by plowed snow in winter.)

If there are no parking meters in sight, you're not off the hook. The city has started to install new black metal columns about 6 feet tall with a white "P" in a blue circle. Press the "English" button, enter the letter from the space where you are parked, then pay with cash or a credit card, following instructions on the screen.

In addition, check for signs noting restrictions, usually showing a red circle with a diagonal slash. The words LIVRAISON SEULEMENT, for example, mean "delivery only." Most downtown shopping complexes have underground parking lots, as do the big downtown hotels. Some of the hotels don't charge extra to take cars in and out of their garages during the day, which can save money for those who plan to do a lot of sightseeing by car.

PASSES The **Montréal Museums Pass** allows entry to 32 of the city's museums and attractions, and is available year-round. Good for 3 consecutive days, the pass costs C$45 and includes unlimited access to public transportation for the same 3 days. It is sold at all participating museums, at the Infotouriste Centre on Square Dorchester, and at many Montréal hotels. For further information, call ☎ **877/266-5687** from outside Montréal or 514/873-2015 within the Métro politan area, or try **www.Montréalmuseums.org**. It's an excellent deal for ambitious sightseers, but you'll have to spend a little less than the recommended touring times in the bigger museums to get the most out of the pass.

PASSPORTS Citizens of the United States, Canada, Ireland, Australia, and New Zealand need only a valid passport to enter Canada. **U.S. residents** can download passport applications from the U.S. State Department website at **http://travel. state.gov**. Residents of the **United Kingdom** can apply for a 10-year passport by contacting the United Kingdom Passport Service at ☎ **0870/521-0410** or searching its website at **www.ukpa.gov.uk**. Irish

residents can apply for a 10-year passport at the Passport Office, Setanta Centre, Molesworth Street, Dublin 2 (☎ **01/671-1633;** www.irl gov.ie/iveagh). **Australians** should contact the Australian Passport Information Service at ☎ **131-232,** or visit the government website at **www.passports.gov.au. New Zealand residents** should contact the Passports Office at ☎ **0800/225-050** in New Zealand or 04/474-8100, or log on to **www. passports.govt.nz**.

Allow plenty of time before your trip to apply for a passport; processing normally takes 3 weeks, but can take longer during busy periods (especially spring). And keep in mind that if you need a passport in a hurry, you'll pay a higher processing fee.

Always make a copy of your passport's information page and keep it separate from your passport in case of loss or theft. For emergency passport replacement, contact your country's embassy or consulate (see "Consulates and Embassies," on p 150).

POLICE   Call ☎ **911** for the police. Most local police speak both French and English, and members of the RCMP (Royal Canadian Mounted Police) are required to be bilingual.

SAFETY   Montréal is one of the safest cities in North America. There are pickpockets and muggings, but they occur with much less frequency than in most major cities of similar size. That said, it's best to stay out of the larger parks at night, for example, and to call for a taxi when returning from a late dinner or a club located in seedier areas. Exercise the same precautions you would in any city and you should do fine.

SENIOR TRAVELERS   Travelers over the age of 65 are usually entitled to discounts in many, if not all Québec museums, theaters, and attractions, as well as on the Métro system. In addition, many Montréal hotels offer discounts to seniors.

SMOKING   Smoking is legally banned in restaurants and bars, but many bars and nightclubs don't prevent people from lighting up. Restaurants either provide non-smoking sections or forbid it altogether.

SPECTATOR SPORTS   Montréal hockey and football fans are a loyal bunch, so attending a home game can be quite an uplifting experience.

The city's beloved NHL **Montréal Canadiens** (☎ **514/932-2582;** www.canadiens.com) have won the Stanley Cup 24 times, though they haven't been major contenders of late. You'd never know that from the attendance at games—devoted fans constantly pack the Centre Bell to cheer on Les Habitants.

There's no denying the loud enthusiasm of the fans who pack McGill University's Molson Stadium to cheer on the **Montréal Alouettes** (☎ **514/790-1245;** www.alouettes. net), the city's professional football team. The Al's have rewarded that devotion with quite a bit of success, getting to the Grey Cup (the Canadian version of the Super Bowl) a number of times.

TAXES   The sales tax in Montréal is rather high, thanks in part to two different taxes being applied to most goods. The federal government imposes a 7% tax (shown as TPS on the receipt), and the Québec government adds on a 8% tax (shown as TVQ) on top of that.

Nonresident tourists can receive a rebate on both the federal and the provincial tax on items they have purchased but not used in Québec, as well as on lodging. To take advantage of this refund, request the booklet called *Tax Refund for Visitors to Canada* at duty-free shops, hotels, and tourist offices.

TAXIS See "By Taxi" in "Getting Around," p. 148.

TELEPHONES The telephone system, operated by Bell Canada, closely resembles the American model. Calls between Canada and the U.S. do not require the use of country codes. Simply dial as you would to another U.S. city. All operators (dial ☎ 00 to get one) speak French and English, and respond in the appropriate language as soon as callers speak to them. Pay phones (found all over the city) require C25¢ for a 3-minute local call. Directory information calls (dial ☎ 411) are free of charge. Both local and long-distance calls usually cost more from hotels—sometimes a lot more, so check.

TICKETS Most tickets for concerts and sporting events in Montréal are only sold through **Admission** (☎ 514/790-1245; www.admission. com), a division of Ticketmaster. To skirt the service's outrageous fees, try to buy tickets from the box office at the venue hosting the event you wish to attend. For performances in some places, such as the Centaur Theater, you can only purchase tickets from the box office or the venue's website. Your best bet is to call each venue for specific ticket information before you purchase.

TIPPING A standard 15% should be given for passable service in restaurants, but bump that up to 20% if the service was excellent. Taxi drivers, hair dressers, and barbers should receive 10% to 15%. Tip C$1 per bag for porters, and C$1 per night for the hotel room attendant. Hotel doormen should be tipped for calling a taxi or other services.

TOILETS The "underground city" not only provides shelter from the weather, but clean public bathrooms as well. Most of the complexes within the city have food courts or shopping centers with restrooms. In a pinch, most restaurants are kind enough to let passing tourists use their bathrooms (though some may require that you purchase something first).

TOURIST OFFICES The main tourist office is the **Infotouriste Centre** at 1001 rue du Square Dorchester (☎ 877/266-5687 from Canada and U.S. or ☎ 514/873-2015; www. bonjourQuébec.com). Accessible from the Peel Métro stop, the office is open from late June to early September from 8:30am to 7:30pm and early September through May from 9am to 5pm. It's closed on Christmas, New Year's Day, and Easter Sunday.

The city has its own convenient Montréal-specific **information bureau** in Vieux-Montréal (174 rue Notre-Dame near Place Jacques Cartier; ☎ 514/871-1595). It's open daily 9am to 7pm from June to mid-October, and 9am to 5pm mid-October through May.

TOURS For a complete listing of tours and tour operators in Montréal, check under "Guided Tours" in the annually revised *Montréal Tourist Guide*, available at **Infotouriste Centre** (☎ 877/266-5687 or 514/873-2015; www.bonjourQuébec.com).

Gray Line de Montréal (☎ 514/934-1222; www.coachcanada-Montréal.com) runs a variety of city orientation and special-interest tours. A basic 3-hour city tour costs C$35.

The most romantic way to tour the city is by **calèches** (☎ 514/934-6105), which are horse-drawn open carriages whose drivers serve as guides. This year-round option (in winter, the horses are hooked up to sleighs), costs C$45 for 30 minutes, C$75 for an hour.

Le Bateau-Mouche (☎ 800/361-9952 or 514/849-9952; www. bateau-mouche.com) is an air-conditioned, glass-enclosed vessel reminiscent of those on the Seine in Paris. It plies the St. Lawrence River, providing sweeping views of the city, Mont-Royal, the St. Lawrence, and its islands from mid-May to mid-October. A 60-minute excursion costs C$17.

TRAVELERS WITH DISABILITIES Aside from the Métro system, most of Montréal is easily accessible for travelers with disabilities. Curb cuts and ramps are found in the busiest parts of the city, and many restaurants and attractions have ramps and specially equipped bathrooms. Unfortunately, the 18th- and 19th-century buildings

of Vieux-Montréal are, for the most part, difficult to access.

Advice for travelers with physical limitations is provided in a French-language brochure, *Le Québec accessible*. It lists over 1,000 hotels, restaurants, theaters, and museums. The price is C$19.95 (US$17.35) from Kéroul, 4545 av. Pierre de Coubertin, P.O. Box 1000, Station M, Montréal, Québec H1V 3R2 (☎ **514/252-3104;** www.keroul.qc.ca). Also look for the Tourist and Leisure Companion Sticker (T.L.C.S.) at tourist sites; it designates that companions of disabled people can enter for free.

A Brief **History**

1535 Jacques Cartier sails up the St. Lawrence and arrives at the village of Hochelaga.

1639 First European settlement established on the Island of Montréal.

1642 The mission "Ville-Marie" is founded by Paul de Chomedy de Maisonneuve, who installs a wood cross at the top of Mont Royal.

1670 Hudson Bay Company is born. The fur trade in Quebec heightens tension between France and England.

1759 The British enter Montréal.

1760 Montréal falls to the British.

1763 The king of France cedes all of Canada to the king of England in the Treaty of Paris.

1775 Montréal is occupied by American Revolutionary forces who withdraw after a few months, when an attempted siege of nearby Québec City by Benedict Arnold fails.

1778 First issue of the *Gazette* (Montréal's first newspaper) printed in French.

1796 The Montréal Library is founded.

1801 The walls that once surrounded the city are brought down.

1812 Americans declare war on England, and the War of 1812 spreads to Canada.

1817 The Bank of Montréal is founded.

1821 English-speaking McGill University receives a Royal Charter and is established in city.

1824 The Lachine Canal is built.

1833 Jacques Viger becomes the first mayor of Montréal.

1844 Canada's Parliament is established in Montréal (Place Youville), though it later moves to Ottawa.

1852 Over a thousand homes are razed by the Great Montréal Fire.

1859 Victoria Bridge is completed.

1924 A new, illuminated cross is unveiled on Christmas Day.

1925 The Seagram Company is founded in Montréal.

1962 City begins construction of the Métro system. The Underground City is born, with the construction of Place Ville-Marie.

1967 The Montréal World Exposition (Expo '67) is held, just as the Métro is opened to the public.

1972 Largest labor strike in Canada's history takes place in Montréal (Common Front walkout).

1976 Montréal hosts the athletically successful but financially disastrous Summer Olympics.

1992 Montréal celebrates its 350th birthday.

1998 An ice storm cripples the city, cutting off power to many citizens and causing millions of dollars in damage.

2002 The 28 towns and cities on Montréal Island are merged into one megacity with a population of 1.8 million inhabitants.

2004 In Montréal, 15 of the boroughs vote to de-merge from the megacity imposed in 2002.

The Politics of **Language**

The defining dialectic of Canadian life is language, the thorny issue that has long threatened to tear the country apart. Many Québécois believe that a separate independent state is the only way to maintain their culture in the face of the Anglophone ocean that surrounds them. The role of Québec within the Canadian federation has long been the most debated and volatile issue in Canadian politics.

One attempt to smooth ruffled Francophone fur was made in 1969, when federal legislation stipulated that all services were henceforth to be offered in both English and French, in effect declaring the nation bilingual. That didn't long assuage militant Québécois. Having made the two languages equal in the rest of the country, they undertook to guarantee the primacy of French in their own province. To prevent dilution by newcomers, the children of immigrants are required to enroll in French-language schools, even if

English or a third language is spoken in the home. Bill 101 was passed in 1977, which all but banned the use of English on public signage. Stop signs now read ARRET, a word that actually refers to a stop on a bus or train route. (Even in France, the red signs read STOP, but then, Québécois like to believe they speak a purer—by which they mean older—form of the language than is spoken in the mother country today.) The bill funded the establishment of enforcement units, virtual language police who let no nit go unpicked.

The resulting backlash provoked the flight of an estimated 400,000 Anglophones to other parts of Canada. Canadian Prime Minister Brian Mulroney met with the 10 provincial premiers in April 1987 at a retreat at Québec's Meech Lake to cobble together a collection of constitutional reforms. The Meech Lake Accord, as it came to be known, addressed a variety of issues, but most important to the Québécois it recognized Québec as a "distinct society" within the federation. In the end, however, Manitoba and Newfoundland failed to ratify the accord by the June 23, 1990, deadline. As a result, support for the secessionist cause burgeoned in Québec, fueled by an election that firmly placed the separatist Parti Québécois in control of the provincial government. A referendum, held in 1995, was narrowly won by those Québec residents who favored staying within the union, but the vote settled nothing. The issue continues to divide families and dominate political discourse.

In the midst of the unshakable fray, Québec remains committed to ensuring, one way or another, the survival of the province's culture and language, its bedrock loyalty to its Gallic roots. France may have relinquished control of Québec in 1763, but its influence, after its century and a half of rule, remains powerful to this day. The Québécois continue to look across the Atlantic for inspiration in fashion, food, and the arts. Culturally and linguistically, it is that tenacious French connection that gives the province its special character, a source of great regional pride and considerable national controversy.

There are reasons for the festering intransigence of the Québécois, about 240 years' worth. After what they unfailingly call "The Conquest," their English rulers made a few concessions to French-Canadian pride, including allowing them a Gallic version of jurisprudence. But a kind of linguistic exclusionism prevailed, with wealthy Scottish and English bankers and merchants denying French-Canadians access to upper levels of business and government. The present strife, and the frequent foolishness and small-mindedness that attends it on both sides, is as much payback as it is pride in the French heritage.

None of this should deter potential visitors. The Québécois are exceedingly gracious hosts. While Montréal may be the largest French-speaking city outside Paris, most Montréalers grow up speaking both French and English, switching effortlessly from one language to the other as the situation dictates. Telephone operators go from French to English the instant they hear an English word out of the other party, as do most store clerks, waiters, and hotel staff.

Useful Phrases & Menu Terms

It's amazing how often a word or two of halting French will change your hosts' disposition. At the very least, try to learn basic greetings, and—above all—the life-raft phrase, *Parlez-vous anglais?* ("Do you speak English?")

Useful Words & Phrases

ENGLISH	FRENCH	PRONUNCIATION
Yes/No	Oui/Non	wee/noh
Okay	D'accord	dah-core
Please	S'il vous plaît	seel voo play
Thank you	Merci	mair-see
You're welcome	De rien	duh ree-ehn
Hello (during daylight)	Bonjour	bohn-jhoor

ENGLISH	FRENCH	PRONUNCIATION
Good evening	Bonsoir	bohn-*swahr*
Goodbye	Au revoir	o ruh-*vwahr*
What's your name?	Comment vous appellez-vous?	kuh-*mahn* voo za-pell-ay-voo?
My name is	Je m'appelle	*jhuh* ma-pell
How are you?	Comment allez-vous?	kuh-*mahn* tahl-ay-voo?
So-so	Comme ci, comme ça	kum-*see*, kum-*sah*
I'm sorry/Excuse me	Pardon	pahr-*dohn*
Do you speak English?	Parlez-vous anglais?	par-lay-*voo* zahn-*glay?*
I don't speak French	Je ne parle pas français	jhuh ne parl pah frahn-*say*
I don't understand	Je ne comprends pas	jhuh ne kohm-*prahn* pas
Where is . . . ?	Où est . . . ?	ooh eh . . . ?
Why?	Pourquoi?	poor-*kwah?*
here/there	ici/là	ee-*see*/lah
left/right	à gauche/à droite	a goash/a drwaht
straight ahead	tout droit	too drwah
I want to get off at . . .	Je voudrais descendre à . . .	jhe voo-*dray* day-son-drah ah . . .
airport	l'aéroport	lair-o-*por*
bridge	pont	pohn
bus station	la gare d'autobus	lah gar duh aw-toh-*boos*
bus stop	l'arrêt de bus	lah-*ray* duh boohss
cathedral	cathedral	ka-tay-*dral*
church	église	ay-*gleez*
hospital	l'hôpital	low-pee-*tahl*
museum	le musée	luh mew-*zay*
police	la police	lah po-*lees*
one-way ticket	aller simple	ah-*lay* sam-pluh
round-trip ticket	aller-retour	ah-*lay* re-*toor*
ticket	un billet	uh *bee*-yay
toilets	les toilettes	lay twa-*lets*

In Your Hotel

ENGLISH	FRENCH	PRONUNCIATION
bathtub	une baignoire	ewn bayn-*nwar*
hot and cold water	l'eau chaude et froide	low showed ay fwad
Is breakfast included?	Déjeuner inclus?	day-jheun-*ay* ehn-*klu?*
room	une chambre	ewn *shawm*-bruh
shower	une douche	ewn dooch
sink	un lavabo	uh la-va-*bow*

The Calendar

ENGLISH	FRENCH	PRONUNCIATION
Sunday	dimanche	dee-*mahnsh*
Monday	lundi	luhn-*dee*

ENGLISH	FRENCH	PRONUNCIATION
Tuesday	mardi	mahr-*dee*
Wednesday	mercredi	mair-kruh-*dee*
Thursday	jeudi	jheu-*dee*
Friday	vendredi	vawn-druh-*dee*
Saturday	samedi	sahm-*dee*
yesterday	hier	ee-*air*
today	aujourd'hui	o-jhord-*dwee*
this morning/this afternoon	ce matin/cet après-midi	suh ma-*tan*/set ah-preh mee-*dee*
tonight	ce soir	suh *swahr*
tomorrow	demain	de-*man*

Food, Menu & Cooking Terms

ENGLISH	FRENCH	PRONUNCIATION
I would like	Je voudrais	jhe voo-*dray*
to eat	manger	mahn-*jhay*
Please give me	Donnez-moi, s'il vous plaît	doe-nay-*mwah*, seel voo play
a bottle of	une bouteille de	ewn boo-*tay* duh
a cup of	une tasse de	ewn tass duh
a glass of	un verre de	uh vair duh
a cocktail	un apéritif	uh ah-pay-ree-*teef*
the check/bill	l'addition/la note	la-dee-see-*ohn*/la noat
a knife	un couteau	uh koo-*toe*
a napkin	une serviette	ewn sair-vee-*et*
a spoon	une cuillère	ewn kwee-*air*
a fork	une fourchette	ewn four-*shet*
fixed-price menu	un menu	uh may-*new*
Is the tip/service included?	Est-ce que le service est compris?	ess-ke luh ser-*vees* eh com-*pree*?
Waiter!/Waitress!	Monsieur!/Mademoiselle!	mun-*syuh*/mad-mwa-*zel*
wine list	une carte des vins	ewn cart day van
appetizer	une entrée	ewn en-*tray*
main course	un plat principal	uh plah pran-see-*pahl*
tip included	service compris	sehr-*vees* cohm-*pree*
tasting/chef's menu	menu dégustation	may-*new* day-gus-ta-see-*on*

Numbers

ENGLISH	FRENCH	PRONUNCIATION
0	**zéro**	*zeh*-roh
1	**un**	uhn
2	**deux**	duh
3	**trois**	twah
4	**quatre**	*kah*-truh
5	**cinq**	sank
6	**six**	seess
7	**sept**	set

ENGLISH	FRENCH	PRONUNCIATION
8	huit	weet
9	neuf	nuhf
10	dix	deess
11	onze	ohnz
12	douze	dooz
13	treize	trehz
14	quatorze	kah-torz
15	quinze	kanz
16	seize	sez
17	dix-sept	deez-set
18	dix-huit	deez-weet
19	dix-neuf	deez-noof
20	vingt	vehn
30	trente	trahnt
40	quarante	kah-rahnt
50	cinquante	sang-kahnt
100	cent	sahn
1,000	mille	meel

Toll-Free Numbers & Websites

Airlines

AER LINGUS
☎ 800/474-7424 in the U.S.
☎ 01/886-8888 in Ireland
www.aerlingus.com

AIR CANADA
☎ 888/247-2262
www.aircanada.ca

AIR NEW ZEALAND
☎ 0800/737-767 in New Zealand
www.airnewzealand.com

AIRTRAN AIRLINES
☎ 800/247-8726
www.airtran.com

AMERICAN AIRLINES
☎ 800/433-7300
www.aa.com

ATA AIRLINES
☎ 800/I-FLY-ATA
www.ata.com

BRITISH AIRWAYS
☎ 800/247-9297
☎ 0345/222-111 or 0845/77-333-77
in Britain
www.british-airways.com

CONTINENTAL AIRLINES
☎ 800/525-0280
www.continental.com

DELTA AIR LINES
☎ 800/221-1212
www.delta.com

FRONTIER AIRLINES
☎ 800/432-1359
www.frontierairlines.com

NORTHWEST AIRLINES
☎ 800/225-2525
www.nwa.com

QANTAS
☎ 800/227-4500 in the U.S.
☎ 13 13 13 in Australia
www.qantas.com

SOUTHWEST AIRLINES
☎ 800/435-9792
www.southwest.com

UNITED AIRLINES
☎ 800/241-6522
www.united.com

US AIRWAYS
☎ 800/428-4322
www.usairways.com

Car Rental Agencies

ADVANTAGE
☎ *800/777-5500*
www.advantage.com

ALAMO
☎ *800/327-9633*
www.goalamo.com

AVIS
☎ *800/331-1212 in the continental U.S.*
☎ *800/TRY-AVIS in Canada*
www.avis.com

BUDGET
☎ *800/527-0700*
www.budget.com

DOLLAR
☎ *800/800-4000*
www.dollar.com

ENTERPRISE
☎ *800/325-8007*
www.enterprise.com

HERTZ
☎ *800/654-3131*
www.hertz.com

NATIONAL
☎ *800/CAR-RENT*
www.nationalcar.com

THRIFTY
☎ *800/367-2277*
www.thrifty.com

Major Hotel & Motel Chains

BEST WESTERN INTERNATIONAL
☎ *800/528-1234*
www.bestwestern.com

COMFORT INNS
☎ *800/228-5150*
www.hotelchoice.com

CROWNE PLAZA HOTELS
☎ *888/303-1746*
www.crowneplaza.com

DELTA HOTELS & RESORTS
☎ *877/814-7706*
www.deltahotels.com

DAYS INN
☎ *800/325-2525*
www.daysinn.com

EMBASSY SUITES
☎ *800/EMBASSY*
www.embassysuites.com

FAIRMONT HOTELS
☎ *800/257-7544*
www.fairmont.com

FOUR SEASONS
☎ *800/819-5053*
www.fourseasons.com

HILTON HOTELS
☎ *800/HILTONS*
www.hilton.com

HOLIDAY INN
☎ *800/HOLIDAY*
www.ichotelsgroup.com

HOWARD JOHNSON
☎ *800/654-2000*
www.hojo.com

HYATT HOTELS & RESORTS
☎ *800/228-9000*
www.hyatt.com

INTER-CONTINENTAL HOTELS & RESORTS
☎ *888/567-8725*
www.ichotelsgroup.com

LOEWS HOTELS
☎ *800/23LOEWS*
www.loewshotels.com

MARRIOTT HOTELS
☎ *800/228-9290*
www.marriott.com

OMNI
☎ *800/THEOMNI*
www.omnihotels.com

RADISSON HOTELS INTERNATIONAL
☎ *800/333-3333*
www.radisson.com

RITZ-CARLTON
☎ *800/241-3333*
www.ritzcarlton.com

SHERATON HOTELS & RESORTS
☎ *800/325-3535*
www.sheraton.com

WESTIN HOTELS & RESORTS
☎ *800/937-8461*
www.westin.com

WYNDHAM HOTELS & RESORTS
☎ *800/822-4200 in Continental U.S. and Canada*
www.wyndham.com

Index

See also Accommodations and Restaurant indexes, below.

Photo **Credits**

Explore over 3,500 destinations.

TOKYO 7766 miles
LONDON 3818 miles
TORONTO 4682 miles
SYDNEY 5087 miles
NEW YORK 4947 miles
LOS ANGELES 2556 miles
HONG KONG 5638 miles

Frommers.com makes it easy.

Find a destination. ✓ Book a trip. ✓ Get hot travel deals.
Buy a guidebook. ✓ Enter to win vacations. ✓ Listen to podcasts.
Check out the latest travel news. ✓ Share trip photos and memories.
And much more.

Frommers.com

The new way to
get AROUND town.

Make the most of your stay. Go Day by Day!

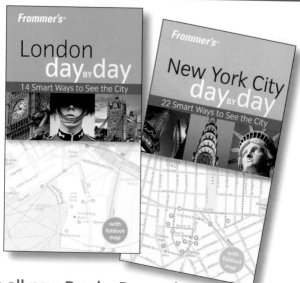

The all-new Day by Day series shows you the best places to visit and the best way to see them.

- Full-color throughout, with hundreds of photos and maps
- Packed with 1–to–3–day itineraries, neighborhood walks, and thematic tours
- Museums, literary haunts, offbeat places, and more
- Star-rated hotel and restaurant listings
- Sturdy foldout map in reclosable plastic wallet
- Foldout front covers with at-a-glance maps and info

The best trips start here. **Frommer's®**

A Branded Imprint of ⓦWILEY
Now you know.